Praise for *Love Lives On*:

"This inspiring book demonstrates that 'mysterious' encounters with the deceased, far from being meaningless hallucinations, are in fact critically important parts of the healing process. Dr. LaGrand shows how we can use these surprisingly common encounters to adapt to loss and return to wholeness."

—Bruce Greyson, M.D., Carlson Professor of Psychiatry, University of Virginia Health System

"*Love Lives On* will be an Extraordinary Encounter or 'EE' for many who read it. It is about the life-changing meanings associated with experiences with loved ones who have died. Talented grief counselor LaGrand not only encourages us to seek that meaning but also shows people how to go about finding it by delineating the role played by symbol, ritual, tradition, and the EEs themselves. Drawing on case histories, in several chapters he describes specific healing and life-affirming approaches to the Mysteries of Life and Death."

—Rhea A. White, Exceptional Human Experience Network, Inc.

"Each year, more and more Americans express belief in spirit survival. According to the Harris Poll, in 2003 a majority—including almost two-thirds of 25–29-year-olds—said they believe in ghosts. In this heartwarming and informative book, Dr. LaGrand, a longtime grief counselor and a leading expert on after-death communication, probes the mystery of sensing contact with lost loved ones and offers a wealth of insights to help the grieving deal with their bereavement. Comfort and wise guidance flow from every page."

—Sylvia Hart Wright, author of *When Spirits Come Calling*

W9-ASZ-790

"Lou LaGrand has probably listened to more stories of Extraordinary Encounters with the dead than anyone alive today. Here he offers hope and appreciation of mystery for the bereaved as he mines those stories for valuable, even life-changing, lessons that they can teach."

—Thomas Attig, Ph.D., author of
The Heart of Grief and past president of the
Association for Death Education and Counseling

"*Love Lives On* is a wise and wonderful gift to persons experiencing loss. Even if you have never had an 'Extraordinary Encounter,' the lessons of the book are a source of hope and comfort—empowering bereaved persons to transform their grief."

—Kenneth J. Doka, Ph.D., professor,
The College of New Rochelle, and senior consultant,
The Hospice Foundation of America

LOVE
LIVES ON

Learning from the

Extraordinary Encounters

of the Bereaved

LOUIS LAGRAND, PH.D.

BERKLEY BOOKS, NEW YORK

THE BERKLEY PUBLISHING GROUP
Published by the Penguin Group
Penguin Group (USA) Inc.
375 Hudson Street, New York, New York 10014, USA
Penguin Group (Canada), 90 Eglinton Avenue East, Suite 700, Toronto, Ontario M4P 2Y3, Canada
(a division of Pearson Penguin Canada Inc.)
Penguin Books Ltd., 80 Strand, London WC2R 0RL, England
Penguin Group Ireland, 25 St. Stephen's Green, Dublin 2, Ireland (a division of Penguin Books Ltd.)
Penguin Group (Australia), 250 Camberwell Road, Camberwell, Victoria 3124, Australia
(a division of Pearson Australia Group Pty. Ltd.)
Penguin Books India Pvt. Ltd., 11 Community Centre, Panchsheel Park, New Delhi—110 017, India
Penguin Group (NZ), Cnr. Airborne and Rosedale Roads, Albany, Auckland 1310, New Zealand
(a division of Pearson New Zealand Ltd.)
Penguin Books (South Africa) (Pty.) Ltd., 24 Sturdee Avenue, Rosebank, Johannesburg 2196,
South Africa

Penguin Books Ltd., Registered Offices: 80 Strand, London WC2R 0RL, England

This book is an original publication of The Berkley Publishing Group.

Copyright © 2006 by Louis LaGrand, Ph.D.
Cover photography copyright © by Ken Graham/Stone/Getty Images.
Cover design by Elaine Groh.
Text design by Tiffany Estreicher.

PRINTING HISTORY
Berkley trade paperback edition / November 2006

Library of Congress Cataloging-in-Publication Data

LaGrand, Louis
   Love lives on : learning from the extraordinary encounters of the bereaved / Louis LaGrand.
     p. cm.
   Includes bibliographical references.
   ISBN 0-425-21193-2
   1. Spiritualism. 2. Spiritualism—Case studies. 3. Bereavement—Psychological aspects.
I. Title.
   BF1261.2.L335 2006
   133.9—dc22   2006022015

PRINTED IN THE UNITED STATES OF AMERICA

10 9 8 7 6 5 4 3 2 1

PUBLISHER'S NOTE: While the author has made every effort to provide accurate telephone numbers and Internet addresses at the time of publication, neither the publisher nor the author assumes
any responsibility for errors, or for changes that occur after publication. Further, publisher does not
have any control over and does not assume any responsibility for author or third-party websites or
their content.

CONTENTS

THE SEVEN WISDOM LESSONS

ACKNOWLEDGMENTS

Writing a book is sometimes like being a quarterback on a football team. You may call all the plays, but you can't gain an inch toward a first down without the contributions of many others.

First, I am indebted to all those who have shared their personal experiences with me over the years, especially those whose stories in this book illustrate important concepts for all mourners to heed. Stories have always been potent influences in shaping our lives and in coping with loss. Your willingness to share will continue to give hope to untold numbers of people and carry them forward in the adjustment to their losses.

Next, a very special thanks to all of my colleagues who have read various parts of the manuscript in its formative stages and suggested running a few new plays, especially Tom Toolen, Linda Goldman, Delpha Camp, Harold Ivan Smith, Jeanne Harper, Ralph Rickgarn, Helen Fitzgerald, Gordon Thornton, Dana Cable, Ben Wolfe, and Linda Backman.

And then the help of my agent, Jane Dystel, who patiently and meticulously corrected my miscues, yet told me to keep adding to my playbook. Thanks. To

ACKNOWLEDGMENTS

Denise Silvestro and Katie Day at Berkley: Your work has greatly improved this book, and I offer my humblest and deepest thanks.

Finally, and most important, to my best friend, Barbara, thank you for your trust and confidence, and the freedom to be who I am.

SEEDS OF HOPE

*In three words I can sum up everything
I've learned about life: It goes on.*

—ROBERT FROST

Twenty-five years ago I was teaching a course on bereavement and death at a small liberal arts college within the sprawling State University of New York system.

I was euphemistically labeled the "death man" on campus by some of my colleagues and many people came to me for help in dealing with the aftermath of the death of a loved one. But one person forever remains etched in my memory bank. Sylvia was a sixty-four-year-old grandmother with short graying hair and deep-set blue eyes who was mourning the death of her beloved twenty-eight-year-old daughter. Sylvia was a student at the college, had made an appointment to meet with me, and then proceeded to tell me the following story.

Before her daughter's death, Sylvia had asked her to try to send a sign that she was okay in another existence. Approximately four months later she was taking care of her grandson, helping out by giving him his evening bath. She had told him to stay in the bathtub while she went into his bedroom to get his pajamas. No sooner had she entered his room than she heard him making a commotion, so she tore back into the bathroom to find him trying to climb out of the tub. "What's the matter? What are you doing?" she asked. He blurted out: "I saw a picture of Aunt Jan and she was smiling." Yes, Aunt Jan, the daughter who had died. This little four-year-old had seen a vision of her face, and he was frightened.

When she finished telling her story, Sylvia hit me with the million-dollar question: "Do you think this could have really happened?" She was in search of needed validation as she studied my face, desperately seeking some kind of reassurance that perhaps her daughter had sent her the message she had asked for.

I restrained myself from the typical knee-jerk professional response "It's all in your head." Having been trained in the scientific method to believe that all such occurrences were illusions or hallucinations, I gulped, paused for a moment, and somehow came out with, "I think it's possible." To be sure, this was not my scientific training talking. Yet, I was strangely confident that I had said the right thing. In effect, my experience with this graying grandmother was the beginning of my twenty-five-year search for as much information as possible from colleagues and clients alike about what I call Extraordinary Encounters* (some people call them spiritual experiences). I was soon to discover that what happened to Sylvia was not an isolated case.

Fast-forward eighteen years later. After interviewing scores of people who had had Extraordinary Encounters (EEs), a friend suggested that I start going back to the people who had shared their stories with me in the first few years of my research to see if there were any positive long-term aftereffects. Of course, I decided to start with the first client who had shared her saga with me. On a return visit to the college to teach in summer school (I had since moved to another job), I contacted her and asked her my million-dollar question: "Did the experience you had with your grandson help you through the years in any way?"

---

*Those of you who have read my earlier books will notice I am using the term *Extraordinary Encounters* instead of *Extraordinary Experiences*. This is merely an attempt to highlight the unexpected nature of the experience for the mourner, and to emphasize it as an integral part of the grief process for some, as well as an overlooked resource for coping with the death of a loved one.

This woman was now eighty-two years old and her response, although I would hear it from others in subsequent years, surprised me. Without a moment of hesitation she said emphatically, "It strengthened my faith." Her belief in the invisible had soared. It had given her the will and determination to move forward with the loving memory of her daughter's gift and to reinvest in life. That answer confirmed my long-held suspicions that Extraordinary Encounters are not one-time episodes that fade over time, but are major forces that last and often change the course of one's life.

Extraordinary Encounters come in a variety of forms and colors, from visions and apparitions to sensing the presence or hearing the voice of the deceased. In some cases, the grieving survivor experiences powerful dream visitations. There are also many so-called coincidences or synchronicities that occur—what Deepak Chopra, in *The Spontaneous Fulfillment of Desire*, calls "the conspiracy of improbabilities." These unexpected events readily reassure mourners that there is something beyond this life and that they are part of something bigger, a larger unknown plan. Anyone can learn to trust coincidences and synchronicities since they point to positive change.

Messages are also received through touch, smell, a third party who often is not a primary mourner (as with the four-year-old), along with a variety of informative symbolic signs. Significantly, all these contacts are *spontaneous* in nature, occurring without warning. The mourner has not actively sought these responses from the deceased. Furthermore, they are not products of magical thinking, nor do they involve the intercession of a psychic.

To the recipient of an Extraordinary Encounter, there is no doubt that it is the loved one or an Intelligent Power who has provided the riveting communication; the signs or visions emerge unbidden from an enormous reservoir of wisdom and insight far beyond our earthbound comprehension. In the midst of their welcome encounters, recipients are at a loss for words to describe the full impact of the experience.

I've had the privilege to witness the results of many profound events that have brought comfort to grieving survivors. This book will highlight the crucial importance of mystery, symbol, ritual, and tradition—integral elements of our existence on this planet—that are commonly brushed aside and ignored in the incessant, infernal clamor of the twenty-first century.

From my perspective, Extraordinary Encounters bring about healing and expanded consciousness for mourners; they tap into a multidimensional realm that has been victimized by the technological revolution. Time and again, in the face of wrenching change, they give meaning to life and counterbalance the often-held view that Western culture is drifting toward disunity and a primarily physical orientation.

There are two goals for this book: (1) to share the insights that can be gleaned from those who have had Extraordinary Encounters while mourning their deceased loved ones and (2) to urge you to use this inner wisdom and what it suggests as an assist to adapt to any loss or change that you encounter on your journey to wholeness. You will discover how to develop a strong inner life, see death as a door instead of a wall, reinvest in life, and find joy once again.

The accounts of Extraordinary Encounters that are detailed in this book are true and are presented as shared with the author over the years. Some names have been changed or not listed to protect privacy as requested. The stories highlight practical lessons to be learned from a thoughtful, unbiased study of these experiences. And although they may be controversial in the eyes of the scientific observer, evidence clearly shows that this inspiring phenomenon invariably leads to personal growth and an expanded and fulfilling perspective on the mystery of life and death.

—Louis LaGrand
Venice, Florida

CHAPTER ONE

WE ARE ALWAYS IN THE EMBRACE OF MYSTERY

Who am I? Where have I come from? Where am I going?—are not questions with an answer, but questions that open us up to new questions which lead us deeper into the unspeakable mystery of existence.

—HENRI NOUWEN

I was twenty-seven years old when my mother died. A couple of years later one of my five brothers was killed in his airplane. That was another hard experience for me. Recently he and his wife had stayed with my husband and me for a week. After they left, I found their pillows, which they had brought with them, neatly tucked under the bedspread. The bedspread was not just thrown over them, which I thought was strange. But as I was getting *the pillows ready to ship, my brother called saying they had left them there by mistake, and that they would turn around and come back to get them. They were many miles down the freeway by then, but he didn't want them shipped. He wanted to come back for them, and asked if I would meet him on the freeway. I did, and after thanking me, he took me and held me for the longest time, then said goodbye. He was killed four days later. At the funeral his oldest son took me in his arms and held me exactly as my brother had and said, "Aunt Leora, this is from my dad." I looked behind my nephew, and there stood my handsome brother, just as big as life. He nodded and was gone.*

Later, I was playing my vibraharp on his birthday. I played one of his favorite hymns and said, "This is for you, Marlin. I so wish you were here to hear it." At that point some little glass bells that hung in our hallway began to swing and tinkle. There was no draft, no reason for them to move, but they did and I know he was there. Again my sorrowful grief turned to a sweet grief. I know those I have lost are not gone; they are very much here with me every day, and their presence, guidance, comfort, wisdom, and support are indescribable and so wonderful.

—Leora West, Salem, Oregon

THE EXTRAORDINARY IS ORDINARY

You may not be aware of it, but almost everyone has had, and will continue to have, hard-to-explain encounters of various kinds. Although denied and often trivialized, the inexplicable is and will always be an integral part of the human condition. Extraordinary Encounters, as I call them, are not exclusive to the spiritually enlightened; they are just as prevalent among skeptical agnostics and die-hard atheists, among common folk and the spiritual elite. People like Leora. People like you and me. But no matter who they come to, and in what form, Extraordinary Encounters help us begin to fathom the complex, multidimensional world around us and its importance for coping with the death of a loved one. And that's what I've set out to do in this book: to show you how embracing that which we cannot explain can lead to healing and renewal.

Extraordinary Encounters are powerful teachers that have the ability to change our emotions and expand our choices for adjusting to loss. They are the conduit to our understanding of mystery, and our connection to a spiritual life we may not yet understand. EEs force us to ask questions like: What is the motive for and the meaning of the experience? What need is it serving? How will I put the lessons to use in my daily life? Where will I go from here? And it's by forcing us to find the answers to those questions that EEs radically change our life views, bringing heightened perception and sometimes even a new awareness of reality.

I've noticed that people who experience EEs almost universally report several insights and lessons. They are:

1. Love is eternal and survives bodily death. Love persists and is renewed despite death, and is given and received through the Extraordinary Encounter. The deceased draw closer to survivors, telling them they know they're in pain and that they wish to assuage it, making the survivors feel acknowledged and cared for. In turn, survivors feel a reinforced sense of love for those who have gone on. The important insight here is: Death doesn't extinguish a relationship; in fact, after death, a new, deeper relationship emerges.

2. Relief and comfort from emotional turmoil is possible. Not infrequently, Extraordinary Encounters radically alter people's grief, as was the case for Leora. Because EEs reestablish a sense of connection, they also restore hope as well as a heartfelt belief in reunion. The recipient becomes more sensitive to the presence of the spirit of the deceased, and finds he or she has a new feeling of peace. EEs bring our consciousness to a new level because they increase our sensitivity to mystery and unexpected phenomena, even as they provide us with guidance. After your EE, you know you are supported and not alone in your sadness.

3. The Self is much more than a physical being. Experiencing the extraordinary reminds us all that we are much more than mere physical beings. Each person possesses an intuitive side, and identifying with that more spiritual side of your persona can often lead to growth and more profound happiness. Many EE recipients reconnect and begin to listen to their innate inner wisdom—perhaps for the first time—and start to ask important questions like: "What is my purpose here?" and "What is the real world all about?" In the best cases EEs start people on their own personal journeys to become more giving and helpful to the world.

4. You can find renewed courage, optimism, and motivation to live. Often, EEs act as energizers, thanks to the new sense of awareness that they bring. It's truly the lack of meaning in life (and death) that's behind much emotional illness. But EEs let us know that there's more to life than the here and now. Suddenly we discover a mother lode of optimism and encouragement that generates a willingness to confront and persist with the problems that follow the death of a loved one.

5. We all have spirituality, if we recognize it. "The spiritual dimension," said renowned psychiatrist Viktor Frankl, "cannot be ignored, for it is what makes us human." EEs can add a new element to our perception of humanity. Suddenly there's so much more to life and death than we previously realized; suddenly we start believing in the non-physical part of life. Spirituality. The Higher Power. The Universe. Whatever you want to call it. The EE sparks our ability to understand the meaning of mystery and the unseen, often rekindling our desire to find a mission in life, a new compass, perhaps even the compassion we thought we had lost.

I define *spirituality*, and use the term in this book, as the many ways we relate to, find meaning in, and live with mystery in our daily lives. For many people, the idea of spirituality is limited, locked away in a tiny, separate part of their lives. But in truth, spiritual moments abound, not just in the form of EEs, but in things such as being awed by a sunset, a photograph, a compassionate act, a beautiful song, or the grasping of your hand by a little child. The spiritual is in everything.

6. It's necessary and good to forgive and complete our unfinished business with the deceased. EEs often allow mourners to let go of the past and move forward, bringing a deep release of emotion and forging new relationships with the ones who have died. As one person said, "The feeling that I have from my experience is that my wife loves me unconditionally. If I need forgiveness for something I feel bad about, it has been given." An EE is often an olive branch, with the deceased either seeking forgiveness or offering forgiveness for whatever transgressions have passed, real or imagined.

Extraordinary Encounters don't only occur when we're grieving the death of a loved one. Often, they arrive when we seem to be at the end of our rope, in the darkness of major life changes. Have you ever noticed how hard-to-explain occurrences pop up to provide us with guidance when we're dealing with serious anxiety-producing circumstances? Whatever the cause, these experiences, these contacts, give us hope for the future and strengthen our inner convictions about spirituality and life, including life after death. They become a catalyst for helping people transform loss into an opportunity for growth. In this book, I'm going to focus on EEs as they relate to death and mourning—but just keep in mind, there are no criteria for an EE to occur.

EXTRAORDINARY ENCOUNTERS AND OUR WORLD

The oral and written records of cultures all over the world give testimony of unexplainable human experiences, dating back to the dawn of recorded history. But the best proof is from your own life. If you look back, I'm willing to bet you'll recall some unexplainable experiences, events you may have offhandedly dismissed, repressed (especially if you were a child, and adults labeled it a fantasy), or forgotten. You see, we've been conditioned to see only logic and finality in the world around us. Science is based on fact and logic—and the extraordinary defies everything logical. Thus, we tend to dismiss anything our senses can't put into linear progression, anything that deviates from "useful" explanations of reality, as wishful thinking, or even a hallucination. Society encourages us to suppress such events, to rationalize our way out of them.

But let me tell you this: If all my years as a certified grief counselor, workshop presenter traveling the country, and facilitator of support groups for suicide survivors, widows, and widowers, have done nothing else, they've enhanced my sensitivity to the reality of a nonphysical world and the fact that we all are touched by it, even if we are not necessarily aware of its implications. I strongly believe that there is a purposeful, Divine Power that comes into our lives in some form. Call it coincidence, synchronicity, dreams, angels, or whatever name you wish, but it is pervasive, intelligent, aware, and continuously reveals its presence as it sees fit.

My work with people who have experienced the inexplicable has also taught me that Extraordinary Encounters come in every possible form—there's no cookie-cutter format. It might be a vision. It might be a familiar scent. It could be something recent, or something in the distant past. In reading this book, you may be jolted by a memory of the extraordinary that occurred much earlier in your life; rest assured, it's not too late to explore and nurture it. I hope you will allow yourself the freedom to experience your own miracle and, equally important, to become aware of and even expect the inexplicable in your life. Believe me when I say that you can learn to become comfortable with mystery.

I want to make this point perfectly clear: You don't have to be religious to experience the mystery of life and death. Listen to what Sylvia Hart Wright, retired professor and author of *When Spirits Come Calling*, told me about her atheist husband. I had asked her if there was anything in her relationship with him prior to his death that might suggest why she and her son had received several contacts from him after he passed on. Here is her answer.

That's an interesting question. The main thing that strikes me is the extraordinary ABSENCE for both of us, before Paul's death, of any interest in the paranormal or belief in survival of the spirit after death. In fact, when my son and I jointly first sensed that Paul was communicating to us, I wondered if, since he'd been such an atheist in life, he was being sent—perhaps in part as a punishment—to inform us that he'd been wrong, that indeed bodily death was not the end of the personality/spirit.

I also must go on insisting that I believe that almost all widows and a great many widowers—providing they have had a close, loving relationship with their deceased mates—feel at least some sense of their mate's presence on occasion after death. There is such a strong taboo against confessing such things in our culture, for fear of seeming crazy or at best hopelessly silly, that many people do their best to deny or explain away any such experiences, particularly as they recede into the past. I also believe that if you "blow off" such experiences, you are less likely to have repeat visitations. Perhaps one major reason why I didn't do so is that I am a very independent-minded person, confident of my own sanity. Also, my first major EE was experienced jointly with my independent-minded, confident son. To add to my son's credentials, in his very demanding high school, he had friends who were interested in and informed about things psychic. Instead of blowing off our experience, I started a log immediately, keeping a record of several odd events that occurred over that weekend during which we had a memorial service for my late husband.

Sylvia's story illustrates the power of surprise and spontaneity in mystery, as well as the importance that we not dismiss Extraordinary Encounters as wishful thinking or imaginary events. As I've said, the human mind has been conditioned to balk at the inexplicable. Yet the fact remains that an estimated seventy million people are convinced that they have received some sign or contact from a loved one who has died or from a spiritual power providing comfort.

But the more important lesson we can learn from Sylvia's tale is that Extraordinary Encounters can touch believers and nonbelievers alike. I have been privy to the personal and mysterious encounters of a wide variety of people. Many of these encounters have resulted in dramatic shifts in beliefs and in the behavior of those receiving them—changes that might otherwise take years of therapy or a major lifestyle alteration to achieve. You see, a big part of recovering from a loss is establishing a new relationship with the loved one who died—one that's sometimes stronger than when the person was alive. EEs prove that the deceased fully expect relationships to continue on another level, even if the survivors think they've all but ended. It's really a matter of us accepting what our loved ones are prepared to give.

Reflect, for a moment, on what Albert Einstein wrote in 1932: "The most beautiful thing we can experience is the mysterious. It is the source of all true art and science. He to whom the emotion is a stranger, who can no longer pause to wonder and stand rapt in awe, is as good as dead; his eyes are closed." And let's also think about something Chet Raymo, Professor of Science and a science writer for the *Boston Globe*, said in his book *Honey from Stone*: "Knowledge is an island in a sea of inexhaustible mystery."

Ramo's observation is particularly incisive in relation to Sylvia's story, specifically the fact that her EEs came on the heels of an absence of a belief in life/existence after death. Where, exactly, did her EEs come from? Nobody really knows. But I want to point out two further observations Raymo makes about knowledge in our high-tech world, observations I believe can immeasurably affect the way people, even nonbelievers like Sylvia, cope with any loss.

The first: We'll always have mystery with us because the growth of the island of knowledge—what we learn—can't noticeably alter the amount of what we can't explain—the surrounding sea of mystery. Once you've opened yourself to the spiritual, you'll likely experience more and more events that don't make logical sense. But that doesn't mean they're not having an effect on your life. And it doesn't mean that you're limited to the experiences you consciously recognized. Just for fun, think about the example of quantum physicists who study the mechanics of molecules, atoms, and subatomic particles. They've discovered there are unexplainable connections between particles that transcend both time and space. When one particle moves, another particle light-years away, perhaps even in the future, moves in response.

Now think about that in terms of your Extraordinary Encounters. Like quantum particles, EEs can impart strength and wisdom at a distance. In fact, the reason Extraordinary Encounters are able to occur is because time and space *don't* limit them. In other words, it doesn't matter how long ago the EE happened—the only thing that matters is how it affects you today.

The second and I think more important implication of

the island metaphor is this: The growth of the island of knowledge also increases the length of the shoreline, along which we will find even more mystery. That's right . . . more and more questions! It's at this shoreline that we will look to find unanswered and sometimes *unanswerable* questions; it's at this shoreline that we will continually find the extraordinary intruding into our lives; it's at this shoreline that mystery, the crest of the wave of learning, becomes real.

The Purpose of Mystery and the Extraordinary Encounter

So far, I've talked about Extraordinary Encounters in terms of the way they open us up to our spiritual sides and teach us to accept and explore the presence of mystery in our lives. But what's next? What, exactly, does mystery do for us, and why is it so important? I've devoted my life to studying and supporting the presence of EEs in mourners' lives because of the life-giving forces of hope, optimism, and possibility they inspire. EEs are truly a reservoir of insight that can be available to anyone who is willing to accept them. They give us peace and hope for the future, and the spiritual strength to adapt to loss and accept the new routines demanded by the changes in our lives. They can give us a new perspective and awareness we never previously experienced. And the belief in the mystery surrounding them will give birth to inner healing, encouragement, and unspeakable awe. As the great English author G. K. Chesterton, in a book titled *Orthodoxy*, suggests: "Mysticism keeps us sane. As long as you have mystery, you have health; when you destroy mystery, you create morbidity. . . ."

I believe hope is the most underappreciated virtue in coping with loss and change. Hope provides us with the strength and wisdom to rise above the emotional and physical obstacles in our paths. It mobilizes our defenses against the gloom and despair that often settles in after a major loss, the time when you feel most powerless, least cared for, and least able to deal with life's jolts. Former President Vaclav Havel of Czechoslovakia, who had been imprisoned numerous times for his protests against the previous communist regime, rightly says that hope "is an orientation of the spirit; an orientation of the heart; it transcends the world that is immediately experienced and is anchored somewhere beyond its horizons." I completely agree. Hope is truly anchored in possibilities, the awareness and acceptance of new ways of feeling, seeing, and doing. You need only gain a tiny bit of hope each day—a single new possibility—and you will win the battle against loss and change.

There's one other concept I want to be sure to touch on before we go any further, one I've used before, but perhaps never fully explained: meaning. I believe meaning is the pivotal force around which life and death revolve. I am convinced that there is no greater human need than to find meaning in what we experience; this quest is at the core of our very existence. Like hope, we grossly underestimate the importance of meaning in coping with loss and change, perhaps because it evades any kind of precise measurement or definition. But make no mistake, meaning is a major factor in health, as it profoundly affects our physical bodies, longevity, as it influences stress levels and the aging process, and of course, the emotional impact of the death of a loved one, as the survivor is confronted with adapting to life without the deceased.

And so, we find ourselves at the beginning again: Exploring and accepting our EEs opens our heart to mystery. Accepting mystery brings us hope. Hope gives us the power to find meaning in a life that might, in the aftermath of the death of a loved one, seem utterly meaningless. Thus, EEs give meaning to loss and death.

I've seen the way EEs can be the difference between coping well with a loss or being mired in pain and isolation. There are untold numbers of mourners who have found more meaning in the unexplainable—the confidence, hope, trust, and love that begin a web of healing relationships—than in any rational or logical experiences in their lives. And that confidence, hope, trust, and love dramatically alters the course of their grief, enabling them to emotionally reinvest in people and purposes.

All it takes is a single Extraordinary Encounter.

THE SEVEN WISDOM LESSONS

Without a doubt, we can never obtain a full understanding of our true nature, or that of our universe, if we rely solely on our physical senses. My hope is that, after you read this book, you will decide to become an explorer of the world of nonphysical reality; you will vow not to underestimate what you can learn from your spiritual side. The world of science is and always will be unable to provide certain answers to your questions about life and the universe. But mystery will always be with us. I know that you can find wisdom by moving beyond what you know to be certain, into the beauty of mystery and what it offers. You can develop a relationship with that mystery and the loved ones you've lost. You can learn to become a better supporter of and friend to others who have experienced loss. You can begin again to feel hope in your heart, and find meaning in your life.

How?

By opening yourself up to the world around you, especially to the spiritual part that feeds the soul, and identifying and accepting your EEs. And by learning and taking to heart the seven Wisdom Lessons you're going to read about in the remainder of this book:

- *Accept Death As a Door, Not a Wall.*
- *What You Focus on Expands.*
- *We Are Not Alone.*
- *Action Heals.*
- *Rebuild Your Inner Life.*
- *Choose to Serve.*
- *You Are Loved Forever.*

Of course, there's no quick fix for grieving or adjusting to loss, and this book alone cannot take away your grief. But it can teach you how you can start to experience less pain and gradually reduce your sadness. As you read the following Wisdom Lessons, remember that, as paradoxical as it may seem, mystery and the hope it can bring are our most powerful weapons against loss. Allow them to become a part of your life.

To do so, it's essential that you break the chains of familiarity that can hold you back. That's what we'll do in the next chapter—seek to break the strangling belief chains about death being a wall.

The road stretches out before us, so let's begin.

You think the dead we loved ever truly leave us?
You think that we don't recall them more clearly than
ever in times of trouble?

—J. K. ROWLING

THE
SEVEN WISDOM
LESSONS

CHAPTER TWO

ACCEPT DEATH AS A DOOR, NOT A WALL

She was further on than you, and she can help you more where she now is than she could have done on earth.

—C. S. LEWIS IN A LETTER TO A FRIEND

ON THE DEATH OF HIS WIFE

Gone or gone on? It's one of the most difficult and most intriguing questions ever posed in human history. Is death the end? Do we disappear, never to be seen again? Or does death herald a new beginning? If you actively practice a religion, whether Western (like Christianity or Judaism) or Eastern (like Buddhism), you most likely have an answer to that question. Or at least, you know what you should believe. But I want to focus on a different source of wisdom, the source we talked about in Chapter 1: the mystery in our own lives.

Most mysteries, including the Extraordinary Encounters we experience, are beyond our understanding. Yet, they emphatically indicate that some part of us does go on, that there is reunion and a world of the spirit. EEs help us understand that death is a temporary separation, a transitional step, a doorway to another kind of relationship between people.

These kinds of stories are happening all over the world at this very moment:

I was raised in a relatively well-off family, although both my parents came from low-income backgrounds. My father was a doctor, and my mom a housewife. When I was two weeks old, my parents hired a lady to help my mom with laundry, housekeeping, and babysitting. She worked for my family until she died, when I was twenty-four. I loved Jenny and we were very close. She was dependable, stable, and optimistic, helping me in ways my mother wasn't always able to. She was also very spiritual and was a deacon in her Baptist church. She was African American and my family is white German Catholic. The only fistfight I ever got into was when I was about six and the neighbor boy called Jenny a racist name. I remember Jenny pulling me off of him and talking to me a long time about how anger never solved anything, and that I should always love even if people were mean. As the years went by, Jenny and I talked about everything. I talked to her about things I never told my parents, and she always respected me and treated me like I was intelligent. When my parents went out of town, I stayed with her and went to her church. She was active in the civil rights movement and even marched with Martin Luther King, Jr., in Alabama. She and I shared a passion for equality of all people. I loved her very much, and she shaped who I am.

Tom (my husband of twenty years) and I met when in graduate school. I had known him only two weeks when we were in my house studying together for midterms. I was deep in my studies when suddenly I was physically "struck" by the realization that someone was standing next to me. I looked, thinking maybe it was Tom, but he wasn't in the room. I want to emphasize that this was such a physically strong sensation that it jerked me up from my studies. I then felt strongly compelled to go outside into the backyard, which I did. As I stood there, I felt a sensation like someone rushing past me and flying into the sky, into the stars. I know this may sound weird, but it was such a strong sensation that it was equivalent to having someone hit your toe with a hammer—I had no doubt. Tom came out and I was in the yard crying. I told him that someone had just died and had come to say goodbye. I didn't know who, and the whole idea was weird because everyone we knew (Jenny included) was relatively young (fifties) and in good health. The next day when I came home from classes, Tom told me that my mom had called. The night before at seven o'clock, the same time I had my "experience," Jenny had suddenly died from no known cause. I think she died from a broken heart, because her spouse of forty years had died several months prior from cancer.

This event changed my life. I know, without a doubt, that we exist after death and that it must be good, because Jenny let me know. This event also changed my husband's life. He has always been incredibly skeptical of anything not scientifically validated (he's a clinical psychologist). He still has no explanation for this event and grudgingly acknowledges that he was awestruck and feels that this event changed his view of life after death.

—Anne, St. Louis, Missouri

Anne's Extraordinary Encounter gave her a powerful message: an awareness and assurance of another dimension of existence after death. It shattered her psychologist husband's firm convictions of death being nothing more than a wall. And for Jenny, the encounter represented one final opportunity to teach Anne a lesson about life and death, to give one last parting gift to ease the pain of Anne's loss. Remember, there is no greater gift than love. And love—or a lack of it—heavily shapes our identities and our lives, as Anne's story makes clear. Many mourners come to realize that their Extraordinary Encounters are, in fact, gestures of love from people who have passed on or from a higher power; they are attempts to prod, assist, or inspire action from a different realm. And that realization—that relationships continue even after death—leads us to renew our sense of spirituality in our day-to-day lives. Here's how one mourner put it:

> *The totality of my experiences since Jacquelyn's passing has created one profound learning for me. This grand learning is the realization that beneath the physical veneer and materialistic trappings of the modern world, we all have a spirit inside. I try not to be too quick to judge people now. We all have life lessons and struggles; they are just different. I try to bring some happiness to someone each day. There is a reprioritization of what is important in life and much of that has to do with relationships between family and friends.*

How enlightening! How wonderful that those who have been touched by the spiritual, who have experienced the extraordinary, can start to see things differently, to make real changes in their lives.

Dr. Barbara Rommer was a specialist in Internal Medicine in Fort Lauderdale, Florida. I interviewed her two months before her untimely death. She was well known for her research on Near-Death Experiences (more on those later) and wrote the book *Blessing in Disguise: Another Side of the Near-Death Experience*. After her husband Sonny died, he appeared several times to people, including her. But let her tell you what happened to Basil, the caregiver she hired for her son.

My husband, Sonny (Salvatore William Pepitone), went into spirit on June 25, 1997. He ruptured an aortic aneurysm that we didn't know he had. He called at my office and said, "I'm in trouble." I rushed home and called 911; everyone was waiting for him (including the vascular surgeon) by the time we got to Holy Cross Hospital. The surgery went phenomenally well, but because of insulin-dependent diabetes, heart disease, his pacemaker, etc., he developed every complication in the book.

Sonny was extremely protective of our profoundly handicapped son, Willy. Even when we had caregivers from Europe, Sonny never trusted anyone with his son.

It was very, very traumatic for Willy to become used to a stranger caring for him after his father went into spirit. But I finally managed to hire a wonderful male caregiver, Basil. He was just fabulous with Willy—kind, gentle, caring, and Willy trusted him. He was with us for over a year.

One day I came home to find Basil looking very strange, very shaky, and very adamant about quitting. He finally told me why. Willy had been upstairs, lying on the floor listening to music, hugging the speakers to his ears so he could feel the vibrations. The intercom was on, and the gate at the top of the stairs was locked (to prevent him from falling down). Willy was fine. Basil was downstairs, watching the TV near my desk, sitting in the big lounge chair. He admitted that he fell sound asleep. What woke him up was "thick gray smoke, so thick that you could cut it with a knife," wafting past his nose. Since he hadn't been smoking, he thought that there must be an electrical fire. He checked every outlet downstairs, every appliance, and even the garage. Then he went upstairs. Willy was fine. Basil checked every outlet upstairs. Then he relocked the gate, came downstairs, and walked into the living room. There he saw, "looking alive and healthy and as solid as you or I," my husband, Sonny. He was standing there smoking a large, long cigar (as he had in life) and gave Basil a very, very angry look "that could kill." Obviously Sonny was angry that Basil was asleep when he was supposed to be caring for our son. I said to Basil: "My husband took loving care of Willy for years. Why would we think that he would abandon him just because he's in spirit?" I tried to convince him to stay on, but he would not.

My husband was one of the galaxy's finest cynics. That is, until he had a profoundly deep near-death experience when he coded in the O.R. That did it. He was no longer the cynic he used to be. His skepticism changed dramatically.

About seven weeks after his physical death he "came to" Linda Vardaman, one of my employees. Linda was obviously shocked to see him, but she was able to say to him: "God, Sonny, why are you here? It's Doctor who needs to see you!" (Referring to me). Sonny said to her: "No, she doesn't. She already knows." It means everything in the world to me to know that he still exists, and especially that he is lovingly watching over us.

I have been researching and writing about near-death experiences for several years. Nearly every one of the people who have them affirms that we absolutely do continue to exist after this physical existence. I had come to believe, really to know, that this is so. But it's just like getting a phone call saying I'd won the lottery. Of course I would want to believe it, but if I actually had the lottery ticket in my hand, seeing the actual winning numbers, then it would be an absolute! Well, all these many things that Sonny, the love of my life, the cynic of the galaxy, has "come back" in spirit to do have been like actually having the lotto ticket in my hand.

Once again the EE has the effect of reaffirming a relationship the surviving member wasn't sure could or would continue after her husband's death. The EE provides validation for the idea that love does live on.

I want to take a moment to go back to those Near-Death Experiences (NDEs), which Dr. Rommer mentions in her story. People who experience NDEs report that, as they come close to death, they leave their bodies and go to another realm, where they sometimes meet those who have predeceased them. Several million people have reported an out-of-body experience in which they saw the operation being performed on them from above (or the accident they were in, etc.), traveled down a tunnel, met a being of light, felt the presences of loved ones, came to a point where they were told they could go no farther, and then were rushed back into their bodies.

The late psychiatrist Elisabeth Kübler-Ross interviewed

a number of people who were blind and who had reported NDEs. As with other interviewees, she asked them to describe their experiences. They not only were able to describe the people who were in the room trying to resuscitate them when they left their bodies, but they also gave detailed descriptions of the clothing these people wore. Imagine, blind people being able to describe in detail things they had never seen! Another impressive NDE example is the Pam Reynolds case. This Atlanta mother was undergoing brain surgery for the removal of an aneurysm, a fragile dilated blood vessel that could burst and prove fatal. Her eyes were lubricated and taped shut to keep them from drying out; she was anesthetized, her body temperature reduced to 60 degrees, and her brain was flat-lined (no brain waves, no electrical activity) in order to facilitate the operation. Tiny speakers, emitting 100-decibel clicks, were inserted into her ears preventing her from hearing during the operation.

Pam experienced the classic features of the NDE: She heard and watched the surgeon using a surgical saw, and saw her grandmother, uncle, and other relatives and friends who had died. Keep in mind that hallucinations are said to only occur in a functioning brain. Pam's brain was far from functional—all the blood had been drained from it. Scientists may wave their hands and dismiss NDEs like Pam's as altered states of consciousness induced by various physiological, psychological, or pharmacological agents, but I believe there's something more to the story.

NDE responders say things like: "To be honest with you, I verbally can't describe it. It's beyond words" or "If I had to put words on it, it was total love, total peace." Others say their experience cannot be compared to anything here on earth. Only one thing seems sure: Most people who experience an NDE or an EE undergo profound inner changes, including a strengthening of a sense of the preciousness of life, a deep belief in an afterlife, a more accepting attitude toward uncontrollable events, a more loving attitude toward others, and a reevaluation of priorities in life. Like EEs, Near-Death Experiences can be a powerful catalyst for belief in the spiritual world.

In my interview with Dr. Rommer, I asked her how her Extraordinary Encounters and her research on NDEs helped in dealing with the loss of Sonny. "I grieved differently," she said. "I wouldn't have been able to function well without them. I even did his eulogy. I could do that because I know beyond a shadow of a doubt that the only thing that died was his physical body. I will see him again. I *know*, not believe. It has also helped in how I deal with my patients," she continued. "It's important for me to help them be accepting of their physical death. There's absolutely nothing to fear."

I want to share one more story from a book called *Hasidic Tales of the Holocaust*. Author Yaffa Eliach tells a moving story of two rabbis, Aaron Rokeach and his brother Mordechai, who were smuggled out of Poland's Bochnia Ghetto in May 1943 by a courageous Hungarian officer. The officer's cover story was that he was bringing two very important Russian generals who had been captured on the Eastern front back to Hungary.

With all the necessary forged paperwork in hand and two clean-shaven rabbis dressed in civilian clothes, the group was stopped and questioned at a checkpoint. The guard would not let them through because he had no record that the "Russian generals" would be arriving. His immediate superior agreed; they could not pass. With tensions rising, suddenly out of the mist, on horseback, appeared three Hungarian generals who ordered the border guard and his superior officer to allow the two captive generals to pass. They did so immediately.

As the car drove off, the three mysterious Hungarian generals saluted the plainclothes "generals." The Hungarian officer behind the wheel was delighted but totally confused—he was sure he knew all the generals in the Hungarian army, but he did not recognize those three. He said as much to his passengers, who just sat there smiling. The rabbis said they knew all three generals very well:

They were their father, grandfather, and great-grandfather, all of whom had been dead for years.

Anne's story, Dr. Rommer's story, and the story of the two rabbis couldn't be more different, in terms of how, where, and when the Extraordinary Encounters occurred. But they all teach us that death is not final, and that loved ones who have passed on not only continue to be present in our lives, but are also actively concerned with our well being and health. Remember . . . death is not a wall. Death is a doorway to a new relationship with those who have passed on.

Which leads me to a question that you might be asking yourself right now . . . is it always a good thing to be in contact with those who have passed over? In most cases, people who are grieving try to temper their sadness with the notion that their loved ones are in a better place. And most often, the signs and messages that deceased loved ones send to their survivors indicate they are happy in their new existence, are whole and healthy, and are free of the bodily pain and debilitating illnesses that might have plagued them in life.

But are there any EEs that aren't loving? Rarely. I've only heard of a few. Some people have been conditioned to think unexplainable contacts are always orchestrated by an evil spirit rather then a loving source. And then there are those who fear a contact from a deceased person who had been emotionally or physically abusive to them in life. Whatever the reason, remember this: Your contact cannot impact you in a negative way if you don't want him or her to. The deceased are *not* watching us every moment, nor do they have power over us unless we choose to give it to them. You are in charge of your own life; you are the only one who has the power to decide what to do with the Extraordinary Encounter you experience, whether to focus on anger and hopelessness, or on building a life of joy and caring. Your thoughts alone are what give or take away power and meaning to otherwise unexplainable contacts.

If the deceased continues to contact you against your will, you can try asking the person what he or she wants. It's possible he might have come to say he is sorry, or offer forgiveness for a past transgression. You can also try invoking the name of your Higher Power—whether it be God, or the Universe, or simply Nature—and command that the spirit leave and not return again. Each night, before retiring, ask your Higher Power to protect you as you sleep. Just as when someone is alive, sometimes boundaries need to be set. In the end you have the choice to accept or reject any contact experience.

ACCEPTING THE CONCEPT OF DEATH AS A DOORWAY

Dr. Rommer was a woman trained in the scientific method, taught in the use of logic and medicine. And yet, she was able to overcome the conundrum facing most people who have Extraordinary Encounters—our own tendencies to write them off as nothing more than illusions, hallucinations, coincidences, or the product of the emotional disorganization of grieving. Certainly, grief was not the trigger for what Basil experienced in his confrontation with Sonny; he'd only been working for Dr. Rommer for a little more than a year. Furthermore, her secretary also received a surprise visit. It would be a real stretch to chalk all those events up to hallucinations.

Don't throw away your common sense in the process of evaluation. If you or someone you know unexpectedly hears or sees something concerning a deceased loved one, put some trust in personal experience. Don't worry so much about what other people—even scientists or trained professionals—have to say about the encounter. When someone tells you, "I was wide awake and my mother appeared to me," *you* decide if that person is sane and trustworthy. And if you or that person decides to seek professional help, stick to your guns. All too often, even therapists discount Extraordinary Encounters instead of building on them. Whether you visit a counselor or a clergy member, try to seek out one who will be supportive of your experience, even if he or she doesn't fully believe in it. Remember, no outside observer completely comprehends what you have personally experienced. Your EE and your relationship with your loved one is one-of-a-kind, and I feel strongly that personal verification trumps preconceived theoretical assumptions.

In short, what I'm asking you to do is to keep an open mind. Anyone who has been so conditioned to believe they have all the answers, all the truth, automatically shuts out an untold number of insights, opportunities, and revelations that would normally flow into their thinking. As Gandhi said, "It is unwise to be too sure of one's own wisdom."

Beyond the general recommendation to open your mind, and use your own intuition and common sense, there are several important steps you should take to help you accept the extraordinary in your life, and work through your grief.

Express your emotions. A critical component of accepting death as a doorway is opening yourself to the legitimacy of sadness and expressing your emotions, to break the conspiracy of silence about death and dying. Remember those old parental directives we all learned as children? "Boys don't cry." "You need to be strong." "Keep a stiff upper lip." Or perhaps even "You want something to cry about? I'll give you something to cry about." Well, forget them all. Emotional expression is part of our very human nature, and we need to explore it in order to fully come to terms with grief. When a loved one dies, a part of your life undergoes a major transition, and your grief is a natural and healthy way of saying, "I love you."

You must learn to accept the fact that it's perfectly normal to have feelings of emptiness, disbelief, numbness, and yearning—feelings that can be very scary, if you've never experienced them before. Know that the full spectrum of responses to your loss may include moments of utter confusion, shock, despair, and feeling deserted, ignored, rejected, or betrayed. Above all, don't be shy about crying. Crying is coping. In fact, I suggest you don't miss an opportunity to cry—it will be good for your body and soul. Crying is at once an act of cleansing and releasing. Your tears will remove some of the toxic byproducts that have built up in your body due to the stress of grief. I promise . . . you will feel better.

If you can't cry or show emotion, it's essential that you

find a way to let your emotional defenses down and find release, especially if you had a conflicting relationship with the deceased. Engage in soul-nurturing arts: Sculpt, write poetry about your loss, draw, paint, or sketch. Work through your grief in your own way. If you feel overcome with guilt and shame because you can't cry as you normally would, I highly recommend joining a bereavement support group at a local hospital or church, or seeing a grief counselor. I often have mourners tell me, "I should have gotten him to quit smoking," or "I should have taken him to the doctor sooner," or "I should have taken him to a different emergency room," as though they did something wrong. But to truly move past conflict and into healing, we have to leave our guilt and regrets behind, whether or not they're merited. Extraordinary Encounters are about moving forward, not backward. A grief counselor can help you come to terms with that fact if you're having trouble accepting it on your own.

Share your grief. This is a crucial survival skill, and a proven way to cope with tragedy, major life changes, and losses. Talk and relate! Even though you may not feel like it, you must open yourself up when you're grieving; you must reach out for support. Talking helps you adjust to the new life you're leading. Sharing grief with others is one of the most effective tools we have for reconciling loss. It's part of the healing process to tell and retell stories about the loved one in life and in death, because talking leads to acceptance. And acceptance of the death, both intellectually and emotionally, is the first remedy for pain. In fact, the refusal to accept loss and remain mired in grief is a major cause of depression. Unexpressed emotions often lead to prolonged mental illness, violence, and even aggression.

Talk about what you have lost. Tell the world what happened to you, and what you are missing. Talk about your regrets, the things you wish you had said or done. Freely cry and rage at the injustice you feel. When the opportunity arises, retell the story of your EE, if you have had one. Retelling the story may bring new insights for action and change. If you aren't a person who can talk to friends or family about your feelings, speak directly to your deceased loved one, to God, or to a professional. Draw or paint them, if you like; certainly you can talk out loud to yourself about them. You may even find it necessary to scream your words, paying no mind to what is proper or acceptable. Remember, you decide when, how, and where to process your feelings and emotions.

It's especially important to talk to people who have received a sign or message from a deceased loved one.

Make every effort to find people who have had the experience, and ask to talk to them. Each conversation alone will be invaluable.

Deal with your excess baggage. Most of us bring excess baggage to coping with our losses—unhealthy attachments, excessive fear of death, poor grief models, rejection from our childhood, or unresolved losses from the past. This baggage can affect the way we deal with our current loss. If you have unresolved losses that you have not fully grieved, now is the time do it. Continuing to bury those losses will only complicate your current grief. If you feel overdependent on others, rejected by an important person in your life, or if you were taught not to show emotion in your youth, make the decision to address those problems. Have a heart-to-heart with the person involved in your distress, or with someone else you trust. Consider joining a support group. I believe the reason support groups are so powerful is because they not only educate and reduce isolation, but also allow participants to express their emotions without holding back, and to realize that they are not alone in their feelings. Group members develop a healing community where all brands of grief are welcome.

Remember: Keeping yourself disconnected from others will prolong your adjustment to loss and change.

Refuse to isolate yourself and close the path to healing. This is especially true if you are depressed. Don't allow your normal reactive depression, which can be caused by burying feelings, real or imagined fears, and anger, to force you to withdraw. (Note that I say depression is normal—by that I mean, the type of depression everyone experiences at times, often after the death of a loved one, not the clinical depression that might well require pharmaceutical intervention.)

Follow your own timetable. Don't be influenced by people who want you to keep your thoughts and emotions to yourself. These individuals might tell you not to cry or carry on because too much grief will make you sick. Remember: Your grief is unique to you. No two people grieve the same way, and it is your right to grieve according to your timetable. You decide the pace of your sorrow, and when the time has come to tell the story of your relationship with your loved one. But even when you do start to open up—when you do allow someone to walk with you in your grief—continue being the authentic you, and set your own tempo for your journey.

I remember reading my father's diary after the death of my mother. He was unable to speak with us about his feelings (so typical of men, although some women follow the same course), but he had written her, telling about how much he missed her. That was his release—I did not push him to say more. Yet by letting out the hurt, he opened up a space inside himself to let the good memories and past experiences come flooding in. No matter how long it takes you, find a way to come to terms with your feelings. Eventually you will arrive at the mental place that an old Navahjo prayer suggests: "Forget not. Remember with a smile."

Don't let yourself get stuck in anger. Anger is a natural response to loss. The problem is, it often goes unrecognized and prolongs mourning, sometimes even leading to depression. All too often, anger is ignored or denied.

Why do we get angry after we suffer a tremendous loss? Because we're struggling to deal with the feelings of lost respect or unreasonable fear. Sometimes, a loss can seem like an assault on our egos. You might find yourself thinking, "Why should this be happening to *me*? Why am I being treated this way? I don't deserve all this pain. What have I done?" For many, it can feel like a slap in the face. Anger is, in fact, partly due to the misperception that we should always be in control of our destiny. Think about that idea carefully—in reality, most of the twists and turns of life are out of our control. When we lose something or someone, we are forced to respond to the reality presented to us, a reality we may not care for.

Sometimes we silently direct our anger at the person who died for something that he or she did in life, or simply for abandoning us. At other times anger wells up in our hearts because of the perceived injustice of it all or what someone did or did not say at the funeral. You may not be aware that you're angry, but take note: Anger could show itself in the camouflage of criticism, fear, withdrawal, subtle sarcasm, intolerance, jealousy, or self-reproach. Or you could be outwardly projecting your anger on to a spouse, a child, a pet, even God. Some mourners feel that their Higher Power was unjust, uncaring, or unfair in letting their loved one die.

To deal with anger, you must seek to understand the motive behind the action that made you angry and recognize human weakness. You may find it useful to remember a time when you were forgiven, as well as the rationale you used when you forgave someone earlier in your life. But all the while, remember that anger is a healthy emotion because it lets us know we are in need. Try to see your anger as an emotional messenger asking you two big questions: "What do I need to do to restore my respect level?" and "What fear or fears of the future do I need to face?" Are you afraid you will not be able to cope with your loss? Determine what needs your anger is telling you to address. That will lead to you doing something constructive, and eventually releasing the emotion. And that will put you squarely on the path to healing.

Decide on forgiveness. This is the corollary to what we just learned about anger. Let someone you trust know of your anger; tell him or her why you are hurting. If someone else is involved in your anger, consider the emotional place that person was in when the transgression occurred. Work on reducing your resentful thoughts and their sources, which could mean severing your ties to negative people. Then rewrite the past by deciding to choose the freedom of forgiveness.

Understand this point very well: Forgiveness is the only real solution for anger. If you can't learn to forgive, you're destined to carry the damaging physiological effects of anger with you for the rest of your life (yes, your life). As University of Notre Dame Professor Lawrence S. Cunningham suggests, refusing to forgive someone generates an internal poison, a malignant force that weakens your heart, drains your energy, and eventually, makes you unable to give or receive love. By contrast, when you forgive, you *open up* the door to love and the acceptance of conditions beyond your control. The Hindu sage

Govinda reminds us that, "We are transformed by what we accept."

Indeed, forgiveness is the release of resentment, bitterness, disappointment, and even depression. It does not mean forgetting, condoning, or failing to find ways to protect ourselves from future hurtful acts. Nor is forgiveness an instant one-act play. It takes time for true forgiveness to work its way from your intellect—you saying, "I forgive"—to your heart—you really knowing you have let it go. If you want peace and better health, and the gifts of love and compassion that we always have the power to give others and ourselves, choose to forgive.

Help someone who is dying. There is no better way to change your fearful images of death than to be with someone who has a life-threatening illness. Even if you spent a prolonged period of time with your loved one as he or she was dying, you can always learn more. There are as many dying styles as lifestyles, and so much to see and understand. Of course, you can't do this while you are fresh in your grief. You're going to need time to heal first—and as we've said, everyone's timetable is different. But at some point, you'll know you're ready.

This also applies for those people who haven't yet lost a loved one. Most everyone will have at least one opportunity to help a friend or family member who is in the final stages of life. Don't shy away—it will be one of the most important learning experiences that you will ever have. Interaction with the dying will give you more insight into life and death than reading a hundred books on the subject, even this one. Each experience will fill you with awe.

One of the most beneficial effects of helping a dying person is that it helps you conquer fear. Those awful images of death you probably have in your mind, the ones you were exposed to and accepted early in life—those are images you can replace. People who are ill or dying have so much to share, so much to give. They teach us lessons about what is important in life, how to choose our own paths.

If you feel that you wouldn't know what to say to someone who is dying, just remember to allow the dying person to be in charge. A hospice physician from Scotland couldn't have said it better when he told his colleagues: "There are three things you need to practice good palliative care: a pair of ears to listen with, a butt to sit on, and a mouth to keep shut." That advice goes for all of us. Dying people want to talk about a lot of things other than their condition. If they express anger, as often happens, *let them be angry.* If they ask you a question, answer honestly. Many people need to be reassured they have fought a good fight, been successful in their family role, and if necessary, be forgiven for real or imagined transgressions in life.

If you're unsure about what the person needs at a particular time, simply ask, "Is there anything I can get you?" or "What would you like me to do?" Be especially sensitive if the person does not want to talk. Just sit quietly and let him or her know you're there. Be a generous listener—often you won't have to say anything at all. When the time does come to speak, you will know what to say—the words will come naturally.

Read books on death and the afterlife. What you believe about the afterlife will affect the way you grieve the loss of your loved one. You can increase your awareness of the idea that the soul survives bodily death. Don't miss reading *Experiencing the Next World Now* by philosopher Michael Grosso, and psychologist David Fontana's *Is There an Afterlife?* The latter will provide the most comprehensive treatment of the subject currently available. Then try Dianne Arcangel's *Afterlife Encounters* and Raymond Moody's classic, *Life After Life.* The information in these four books alone will provide abundant and reasonable evidence that death is transitional, not terminal. You can also try reading my other books, *After Death Communication* and *Messages and Miracles*, where you will find a wide range of different stories of contact from those who have gone on to a new existence. All of these works will help you come to terms with the fact that Extraordinary Encounters are a normal and natural reality for mourners, even though we've been conditioned to believe they are creations of the mind.

Communicate directly with your loved one. Catholics and other Protestant denominations embrace the belief that those who die can be prayed to directly for guidance, advice, even for help. People who are grieving the loss of a loved one—even if they are not Catholic, or don't even believe in a Higher Power—should consider taking that idea to heart. Remember, death in no way diminishes the loved one's value to those who are still alive. In fact, we can still be greatly effected by the deceased's continued presence, and learn a great deal from his or her advice and opinions as we deal with problems. Ask questions, and you will find answers—of that much I'm sure. (Whether or not you agree with those answers is a different story.) Carefully consider their opinions as you make your choices. Soon you'll find insights seemingly coming out of nowhere.

I hope, if nothing else, these nine steps—express your emotions, share your grief, deal with your excess baggage, follow your own timetable, don't get stuck in anger, decide on forgiveness, help someone who is dying, read books on death and the afterlife, and communicate directly with your loved one—help you to be better able to deal with your grief. Increasing your knowledge about coping skills *can* help you through loss, and will have immediate benefits as it helps you realize the normalcy of your thoughts and feelings.

Read. Use the Internet. Do a Google search on "grief," and you'll find dozens of websites devoted to helping mourners, such as www.griefshare.org, articles on grief, and chat rooms. There is so much to learn. Trust and give in to the grief process: It has wisdom built into it.

Everyone has to cope with many "little deaths" before they cope with a big death, including their own. Losses of every kind—from the loss of a home, job, community of friends, or cherished heirloom to the breakup of a relationship or the incarceration of a family member—may bring a strong grief reaction. The intensity of response depends on the degree of emotional investment in the object or person involved. That's one of the major reasons why every person's grief is uniquely different, as are their needs. Not everyone experiences the same depth of emotions, nor do they go through set stages of coping, as some books suggest.

Regardless of the type of loss, it's important for mourners to realize that *it's all right to ask for what you need*: a hug, a shoulder to cry on, to be alone, someone who will listen, or help with daily duties. It's okay to depend on others for a while. Being reluctant to ask for help only leads to additional suffering.

I want to take a moment to talk about one related issue, what I call *secondary loss*, which almost always accompanies major losses. Secondary losses can come in hundreds of different forms: financial (you have to move out of your home), social (you are no longer invited to certain gatherings), physical (the absence of being touched, held, or having sex), intellectual (no one to talk to about topics of great interest), and of course deeply emotional (loss of companionship, counsel, or support). The loss of your dreams for the future, as well as the loss of meaning in general (goals, faith, and joy), can sometimes be even more devastating than the loss of the loved one. It's vitally important that we learn to recognize and mourn these losses as we would any other, without feeling guilty that "we're not over it" or "we haven't yet moved on." Coming to grips with secondary loss is part of the long-term healing process.

It's possible that secondary losses won't surface until months or years after the major loss in question. Even if you feel like you're generally doing well, you may be blind-sided. Say, for example, you suddenly realize your loved one is not with you for your daughter's graduation; you might feel sad and want to cry. Do so. You have every right to mourn every loss related to the major loss in your life.

Whenever I give a lecture or workshop on grief or coping with the death of a loved one, I usually begin with an insightful Chinese proverb well-known in the grief literature. "You cannot prevent the birds of sorrow from flying over your head, but you can prevent them from building nests in your hair." The proverb points out two extremely important concepts. The first: All relationships end in separation, whether due to death, divorce, disagreement, incarceration, or relocation, to name a few causes. And "the birds of sorrow" will fly over your head and reappear throughout life. Bad things happen to all of us; brokenness permeates life, which is unpredictable and at times unfair. As many therapists tell their clients, "the problem with fairness is that it doesn't exist." Nothing you do can give you immunity to the loss of loved ones. There are no exemptions: Everyone dies and walks through the doorway of death. It follows that grief and suffering are forever part of the human condition.

Nonetheless, although all physical relationships must come to an end, our emotional relationships do not. As

I've tried to make clear in this chapter, after death, a new relationship is born: one based on memory, legacies, gratitude, and the fact that love lives on. That's where the second important concept from the proverb comes in, and also the significance of Extraordinary Encounters. *We can prevent sadness from taking root in our lives if we open ourselves up to mystery.* The love we share with the deceased remains with us forever and is expressed through the gift of the EE—as it was for Anne and Jenny, and Dr. Rommer and Sonny. The loved ones in our lives will always strengthen us and inspire noble deeds. Suffering is built into the very nature of our existence, but EEs help us work through our grief and keep love strong.

There is guidance, direction, and order behind all EEs. They represent wellsprings of love and meaning at a time when life is filled with sadness and stress. And sometimes they are dramatically played out. As we close this chapter, let me tell you about a case witnessed by four people.

My wife, Pat, passed away on October 30, 1996, after a long struggle with juvenile diabetes and its many complications. She was forty-nine years old. Pat never let the disease take away her zest for life, which was reflected by her love for me and our children. She always cared more about other people's problems than her own.

She was an inspiration to all who knew her, and her passing has left a void in the life of her family and friends. That description of her may give you some insight into the occurrence that happened in September 1997, a year after her passing.

The people present were my fiancée, Kathy, and Betty and Jim, who were Pat and my best friends. The evening was casual, with about an hour of sitting in the hot tub, which we always did when Pat was alive. Then we went into the kitchen for wine and snacks. The conversation was light, and some mention of how Pat always enjoyed our hot tub evening ensued. We were sitting around a six-foot-long kitchen island, when the empty wineglass in front of Kathy glided across the island like it was on a sheet of ice and stopped in front of me! It had moved at least four feet. No one had touched the glass or in any way caused it to move. There were other glasses and snack plates, etc., on the surface of the island, and the glass never touched any of these. It floated like it was on a sheet of ice, like someone making a movie was doing a superb visual-effects scene.

Everyone just sat there for a moment with bewildered looks on their faces until I said, "Did anybody just see that?" They all said yes, and I think they all had the same thought as I did—that it was Pat. Jim and Betty were at a loss for words and immediately said their good nights and left right away; Kathy and I were shaken, but we knew what we had just seen. There was no fear and we knew that Pat lives on.

We retired to the upstairs bedroom, but throughout the night, Pat's dog was extremely agitated, pacing and whining, and Kathy's cat was acting in a similar manner. The next morning we talked about what had happened, and both of us felt that Pat's spirit had visited us throughout the night. Kathy also related to me that she had gone downstairs during the night to quiet the animals and had felt a strong presence pass by and around her. Several days later I removed Pat's remains from the house where they had been in an urn on one of her favorite antique tables overlooking the living room. I took them to my oldest son's house, where they are still kept.

My wife's gift was that she wanted to make herself known and she did. As a result, I have learned that death is something you don't have to fear. There is a life hereafter.

—*Brad Cummins, Los Angeles, California*

Rarely are our paths straight. They take sudden twists and turns, and invariably straighten again. That's what happens to many mourners who have a contact experience with their deceased loved ones—they start to pay special attention to its central meaning. They discover a seldom-utilized process that few people are consciously aware of: Whatever you focus on expands. We will turn to this powerful coping strategy in the next chapter.

Bemoan not the departed with excessive grief.
The dead are devoted and faithful friends; they are
ever associated with us.

—CONFUCIUS

CHAPTER THREE

WHAT YOU FOCUS ON EXPANDS

The soul is dyed the color of its thoughts. Think only on those things that are in line with your principles and can bear the light of day. . . . Day by day, what you do is who you become.

—HERACLITUS

As I've suggested in the first two chapters, I've been privy to many Extraordinary Encounters over my career as a grief counselor. But over the past two decades, none have moved me more than the following story, a childhood experience of an Australian woman named Diana Sautelle. The life-affirming contact Diana had with her deceased childhood friend is a vibrant example of an important coping technique: the idea that *what you focus on expands*. In this instance, the expansion takes place in Diana's consciousness, in her awareness of the spirit, and in who she was and what life was all about.

First, I should mention that, because the incident I am about to describe occurred while I was a child, I hadn't developed any judgments at all regarding the so-called impossibility (or possibility) of such an experience. But it is because of this experience in particular that I have simply never questioned the idea of life beyond the physical realms. It actually hasn't ever occurred to me to doubt the reality of dimensions that are not fully physically manifest. This is truly how I see the world.

The brief background to this event involves a particularly deep and loving friendship I developed with another child at school—a beautiful, gifted, and artistic boy named Ernie. I was seven when we began our friendship and he was, I think, around nine years old. We had an extremely strong feeling for each other, a deep sense of knowing each other, and our friendship was filled with declarations of love and foreverness. We spent time together at school, and on weekends. We would roam the local paddocks and streets, collecting legless lizards from the surrounding bush, playing, and one time I remember that we "practiced" hugging and kissing for when we were going to be married. Thus, as young children, we essentially spent our time in some type of very naive preadolescent betrothal state—that's about the only way I can describe the quality of feelings we had.

This all went on for about one and a half years, until one night, when I was nine and a half, I awoke in the middle of the night to the sound of Ernie calling me insistently: "Wake up, wake up, quick." I sat up in bed, my eyes open, to find Ernie standing in the doorway of my bedroom. He was laughing with sheer joy and happiness, smiling and beckoning me with his hands to follow him, with the words, "Hurry, hurry, hurry up, quick." There was a sense of urgency and immediacy, which was very intense and insistent.

I could see straight through him to the hallway wall behind him. He was transparent, although very clearly there in all ways, just simply "see-through." Then I saw that the top half of his body and the bottom half of his body were not connected—he was in two pieces, not joined in the middle. But it wasn't gruesome, they just weren't joined. This reduced me to immediate uncomprehending tears, and I called to him, "What's happening? Tell me what's going on." He just kept laughing happily and repeating, "Quick, quick, hurry," as he beckoned me. Then he disappeared down the hallway, and I rushed from my bed and followed as quickly as I could. I could still see him moving down the hallway toward the kitchen. I was calling out, "Slow down, wait for me, what's happening?" It felt vital that I catch up with him. When he entered the kitchen, he turned around to face me, beaming incredible joy from his whole being, a sort of elation of the spirit, and the whole room was full of light. I was so pleased he'd stopped moving, because I had imagined that if I could somehow reach out and hold him, then I would find out what was going on. Meanwhile, I was crying in utter confusion. Everything was happening too fast for me and I couldn't grasp the situation, although I felt desperately that I must try to understand what was happening. I reached out to touch him, asking him to wait for me—but my hands went straight through him. At that moment he began to quickly rise upward, still laughing and smiling at me. An instant later, when he was halfway up toward the ceiling, his whole body disappeared within an intense and glorious spiraling of colors. Inside this rapidly spiraling rainbow of colors and motion, he completely disappeared above me, and I could hear his beautiful laughter as he departed.

I knew that something huge was happening, but as a nine-year-old child I simply stood in the kitchen sobbing as though my heart had broken. Deep inside of me, I somehow knew that I'd lost Ernie, that he hadn't been able to wait for me, and I was overwhelmingly bereft.

I was collected from the kitchen by my father who had heard me crying and who took me into bed with him and my mother. They tried to comfort me, thinking I had had a bad dream. I cried for a long time—for a long time after my parents had fallen back to sleep. The last memory I have of that night before I fell asleep, which was as the sun was rising, I was clearly seeing a transparent and large hand stretching toward me from outside the window into the room.

That day, upon awakening again, I felt numb and shattered. It was late in the day when I heard the news that Ernie had been in a terrible accident at six the evening before. He had been killed in an accident in which he was cut in half by a train. His spirit had come to me and awakened me some seven or eight hours later.

So this is a story of a loved one making contact with me before I knew he'd died. It was many years of deep internal work before I could let go of my own painful loss and my horror of Ernie dying in such a violent way. As a child, I didn't comprehend that he would not have felt the terrible pain of being cut in half, and unfortunately, no one in my life at that time recognized that I needed that reassurance. Eventually through more mature contemplation, I have been able to integrate the significance of Ernie's deep joy, understand that he was completely reconciled with his death, and that I was blessed to have him ask me to witness his prismatic spiraling exit from this world.

I know that this childhood experience was intensely profound and powerful, and carried with it a force that has influenced the direction of my life's journey; it has reinforced my inherent lack of cynicism and my awareness of things beyond the physical realms. I believe in the mystical because I sense and experience this at all times, and I since have had many experiences, although not infused with the same level of immense grief and personal loss. Yet they always contain spiritual information that resonates deeply with my sense of life's meaning.

Aside from the inherent significance in Diana's encounter (that is, reinforcing the fact that death is a doorway, not a wall), there's something else I want you to take from her story: Extraordinary Encounters can very powerfully affect the way you live your life. Diana found wisdom and purpose in her EE that proved to be the seeds of a lifetime philosophy. As psychologist Tobin Hart notes in

The Secret Spiritual World of Children, "Childhood moments of wonder are not merely passing reveries. They shape the way a child sees and understands the world, and they often form a core of his or her spiritual identity, morality, and mission in life." That's why it's so important that we acknowledge and respect EEs reported by children instead of dismissing them as the product of an overactive imagination.

But getting back to the concept of meaning in Extraordinary Encounters . . . Diana's experience with Ernie has influenced the way she interacts with her community. She came to realize that we are all intimately connected—we all are one—and that we all need each other. The EE motivated her to consistently relate to others with a greater sense of love whenever she is confronted with deprivation, poverty, or abuse. Seeing the universe in a new perspective, Diana was motivated to contribute her talents to the welfare of those in less fortunate circumstances. She began donating her time as a volunteer in remote indigenous communities, giving papers and presentations on the issues related to homelessness, domestic violence, and childhood abuse, and mentoring a number of local musicians and artists.

That's what I mean when I say that what you continually focus on in your thoughts expands: You are what you think and how you consistently respond to those thoughts. This expansion can occur on any level of life—physical, emotional, intellectual, or spiritual. But wherever you plant that seed within, it will grow. For Diana's part, after she received her healing gift, she became convinced that she had to cherish it, share it, and make it come alive. The experience came to dominate her thoughts, and became part of her life mission and healing journey. You must recognize that healing is not a finite process. We are always healing in one way or another—it's part of our ever-changing lives as we move from situation to situation, loss to loss.

LEARNING TO FOCUS ON THE POSITIVE

As you can well imagine, it follows that learning to shift our focus and redirect our attention is a critical skill in coping with the death of a loved one. Let's examine that skill in depth.

Once on a trip to the Florida panhandle, I passed through a small town. On a marquee on the main street I saw the following message in bold black letters: WHILE ADDING UP ALL YOUR TROUBLES, DON'T FORGET TO

COUNT YOUR BLESSINGS. What a powerful lesson! That small thought can act as a springboard for developing hope and increasing a sense of power and direction in life. For if we look closely, we'll see that Extraordinary Encounters restore our sense of power and stability in the world by bringing about the realization that there is a guiding force in mystery, and therefore in the universe. Focusing on that source of ever-present care and support can give us great strength.

At the same time EEs can release in the recipient abundant amounts of energy to use in the restoration of life after loss. Diana's experience illustrates the motivation an EE can provide—motivation that she expressed in her volunteer work as well as her own personal growth. Her experience was progressive over time, in the sense that it continually increased her insight into Ernie's visit, and its effect on her life and on all those she assists. This is an example of the profound psychological transformation that can result from Extraordinary Encounters.

I'll be the first to admit—it's not easy. After a major loss most people experience a strong (and very normal) tendency to focus on what they don't have, especially what they've recently lost, and to minimize all the blessings currently in their possession. Believe me when I tell you that that kind of thinking *conditions your mind to think negatively* and, over the long run, only adds to your suffering.

And here is the most destructive part: Anchoring your attention on what you lack is self-defeating, because sooner or later—as you are mourning—it's inevitable you're going to come across something else you can't have. Help yourself in a very positive way by reducing the time you spend comparing yourself to those who still have a particular loved one at their side, or more friends or family nearby to provide support. Instead of obsessing on your loss, try to think about everything that carries on—what you gained from the relationship with the deceased, and what you can continue to take from it. If you're able to take this important—and admittedly, very difficult step—you'll make a big leap in your journey to healing.

Another part of eliminating negative thinking is avoiding our natural tendency to complain. We all have a few chronic complainers in our lives, people who find fault with everything and constantly point out the devastating effects of those faults on life. Remember: Everyone has problems, both large and small. No one wins all the time; no one gets off the trouble train scot-free, even though they may put on a happy face in public. It's just part of the human condition that things don't always go according to plan. Most important, we have to accept that no one has control over death.

I believe there's very little neutral ground between gratitude and complaint. If you stop giving thanks each day for life, love, insight, growth, and health, you are bound to drift toward ingratitude and self-pity, two great inhibitors of healing. But there is good news! As I've said, and as we have seen in stories like Diana's, *what you choose to focus on makes the difference between finding yourself at the end of your rope, or reaching up and getting back into the mainstream of life.* Your attention becomes the source of your becoming, of your growth.

At this point, you may be wondering what specific actions you can take to achieve this refocusing of positive energy. How can we jump-start the search to rediscover how much we possess? There are several simple steps you can take.

Make a list. Get a sheet of paper and draw a vertical line down the center. On the right side of the line, list your problems. On the left side, write down everything you are thankful for—family, friends, health, home, job, skills, automobile, faith, support group, etc. Put the piece of paper away in a safe place; take it out and add to the list as you discover more of your blessings. As difficult as it may be, make every effort to consciously shift your attention to what you still possess, despite your great loss. Read through your list frequently. I promise, that one action will reduce stress and help you nurture the hope that springs from all of the connections you still have in your life.

Watch less TV. Another simple step you can take is to cut back on the amount of television you watch. TV brainwashes people into believing that they should always want more—more money, more material goods, more happiness in general. Even worse, television all too often triggers the painful reaffirmations that our loved ones are no longer with us. You can be caught off guard by scenes showing couples, fully intact family gatherings, or places that remind you of past vacations you took with your deceased loved one. Early on, you're just not ready for those kind of reminders. As an alternative, try playing music—whatever genre you find most moving and soulful, at least until your grief has become more manageable. Several studies have shown that slow meditative music acts as a stress buster and reduces heart rate (that's why many hospitals use it). And music's association with emotion, even prayer, has long been documented. Try making a CD or an audio tape of your favorite slow music; I suggest including some symphonies.

Visualize and rehearse tough situations. One of the most under-utilized secrets to coping effectively with loss and change is to practice handling difficult situations before they arise. How do you do this? Visualization. Visualizing is really nothing more than *practicing and seeing within* what you want to eventually do on the outside. Change your inner images by imagining exactly what you want to emphatically say or do, and you'll change how you respond to the outside world.

So, what kind of situations should you rehearse? You can imagine anything you like, although I believe the best thing to do is to practice the way you deal with worst-case scenarios. By doing so, you'll be able to determine all the possible positive responses you could have before you actually need them. On top of that, when you practice, you'll also reinforce the positive energy that is inherent to choosing to be prepared. You will erase the fears you harbor within, and replace them with words and behaviors that support successful coping.

"See" yourself overcoming fear (for example, the fear of going somewhere alone for the first time) or uncomfortable moments (for example, seeing the family of the deceased for the first time). Rehearse the way you'll combat toxic worry, or the way you'll forgive someone for whom you harbor anger. Be sure to emphasize the *specific positive behaviors* you plan to apply—the way you're going to talk to the other people involved—and be specific in terms of picturing the place, time, your clothes, your demeanor, and the emotional disposition you wish to possess. Practice your plan as you lie in bed at night, or set aside a specific time during the day. Most important, don't criticize yourself if your first attempt at visualizing falters. Go back and work on responding to the stressful situation just as you designed it, until your response becomes automatic, and then use it when the occasion arises in the real world.

Hang a meaningful work of art. Look for a painting or drawing to hang in your home that evokes your lasting connections with the person who has died—something that reminds you that love does live on. Of course, you can always create your own work of art to express your feelings and show your continued love for the deceased. I know an artist who did just that. After the death of her brother, she painted two beautiful scenes, each of which included a portrait of him in the background. If you are not artistic, write a poem, frame it, and hang it in a favorite place that will inspire you throughout the day and help you in your quest to change the focus of your thoughts.

Concentrate on what your loved one taught you. Think of a characteristic, idea, or skill that your deceased loved one brought out in you, or consistently reminded you of, and use it to help yourself and others. Perhaps the deceased increased your gentleness with children—if so, think about volunteering at a day-care center or school. Maybe he or she encouraged you to pursue writing—if so, consider taking a writing class. Think of what you can do to become even more proficient with your abilities and how their development can be a lasting memorial to your loved one, a bridge of love that welcomes the beloved back into your life. Then, put that plan into action.

Create your own affirmations. Your attitudes and beliefs really do affect the way you live your life, and creating affirmations that reflect your goals and the attitude you want to develop will help you cope with your loss. Affirmations slowly but surely chip away at old habit patterns and unconscious beliefs, paving the way for positive healing. It all starts in the mind.

So when you look in the mirror each morning as you start your day, say something positive about yourself. Remind yourself that you *will* prevail. *I will get through this day. I will not break down again.* Most important, put your affirmations in the positive tense. *I am motivated to give and receive love.* To help deal specifically with the loss of a loved one, you might try affirmations like *I am letting go of negative thoughts and accepting the new* or *I am starting new traditions.* Create phrases to use as weapons against each negative thought that plagues you. Write your favorite on a card that you can take out and read when you're riding the bus or the train; record them on a tape to play in your car or at home. Consider including your name. *I, John, am gradually reinvesting in life.* Memorize your affirmations so that you know them as well as your name. Create one for each goal you set for yourself.

Whatever words you choose, when you speak, visualize yourself making good on your affirmation in the real world. Coupling your affirmations with images of what you wish to accomplish will build a link between your conscious and unconscious minds. Relax, say the words, see the picture, and feel the change in yourself.

As corny as they may sound, affirmations have helped millions of people live positive and constructive lives. The key is persistence.

Create a personal symbol. Symbols can provide comfort and guidance, and can help mourners expand and focus their thoughts. It could be a single word—Love, Shalom, Friendship, Yes, Peace, Caring. It could be a picture cut from a magazine, a cherished photo, a toy, or any other object that has special meaning for you. I know a woman who came home one day to find her husband dead from a heart attack. Based on a series of EEs she had after his death, she designed and had a beautiful pendant made by a local jeweler from his and her wedding rings. In her words the pendant was a symbol of "Rick's unending love for me and mine for him!" and a special way to help her cope with her great loss.

Your symbol could actually be an action. Light a candle for your loved one when you're enjoying a family event. Play his or her favorite music or make a quilt from his or her favorite clothes. Wear a piece of the deceased's clothing. Choose a special glass, cup, or plate; take the item to a craft shop and have the name of your loved one or a special phrase etched or printed on it. Create or purchase a special ornament for your Christmas tree. One family had an ornament for every pet or person who influenced their family life, and it became tradition each year to place these visual reminders on the Christmas tree as a way to remember and show gratitude for their positive influences.

Finally you may wish to find a symbol that represents the release of conflict or unfinished business you had with the deceased. Use it to extend an apology, or to imagine what the deceased would have said to smooth over old disagreements. Eventually discard it as a sign of reconciliation, progress, or forgiveness.

Whatever your symbol is, use it as a sign that your deceased loved one is still with you. When you look at it, let it remind you that it's okay to ask for guidance from your higher power or to ask your loved one to intercede for you. Nothing's wrong with saying out loud, "Please give me the wisdom to make the right choices this day" or "Please give me the courage to follow my plan." Your loved one is there and will assist you!

I believe symbols are particularly helpful to mourners because of the way they provide concrete points of reference for beliefs—specifically, new beliefs. It's not uncommon to question beliefs about life, including spiritual beliefs, at a time of major loss. As I've been saying, our biggest challenge at that time is to refocus our thoughts and beliefs on the positive, to reinvent our mindsets. Although we might strongly resist these kinds of paradigm shifts, they're an essential—and ongoing—part of the grief process. As you feel yourself falling back into old mindsets, let your symbol be a reminder to refocus on the positive.

The bottom line is: You will endure—that's the history

of human loss. But how you do it is up to you. Personal symbols can help you keep a close grip on your new beliefs; they can, in a sense, provide grounding for an otherwise totally mental and emotional process. They can generate an immense amount of new energy through the meaning they bring into your thoughts.

Never stop learning. Learning and *doing* new things is a tonic for the mind. Refuse to put limits on the things you want to know. The continued search for learning will keep you positively oriented and help you reinvest in your new world. Become a student of life; life teaches, so force yourself to be receptive to new experiences. Visit new places; I recommend taking a trip with Elderhostel. Take a writing, painting, or crafts class. If you are retired, look for one of the Institutes of Learning in Retirement in your community. Check out local bookstores, libraries, museums, retreats, workshops, community lectures, classes, and seminars to find information tailor-made for you. In your search you will discover that you have more to give to the community that you might think.

The act of obtaining new information and doing new things is itself physiologically healthy for the brain. On a microscopic level you'll actually be adding new brain cells. Furthermore, the excitement of discovery will boost your flagging energy and help you move forward, fight loneliness, and find new vantage points to help you cope with your loss.

Those kinds of actions are concrete steps you can take to become an expert at *shifting your focus*. They represent simple ways of developing rituals for your new life—rituals that fulfill our desire for connection and a sense of belonging, especially when we're mourning. Whether formal or informal, rituals are major tools for reestablishing stability when dealing with transitions of all kinds because of the way they provide support and meaning, establish new traditions and routines, change and/or strengthen beliefs, show appreciation, and provide comfort. In a nutshell, rituals shape and form us in our new life; they are self-care in action.

The new traditions and routines you install through ritual will be especially useful in reestablishing your identity after major loss. I remember one widow who was unable to eat after her husband died. They used to eat dinner at six each night in the kitchen of their home. After he passed, she couldn't bring herself to do it without him— so she started a new ritual for healing by eating at five in the breakfast nook. This simple adjustment changed her grief expectations and became an instrumental step in her adapting to loss. Think of the new rituals you need to develop to take the place of the old that no longer have the same meaning.

So, where do you begin? The answer is: anywhere. Rituals can be conducted in the privacy of your bedroom, in your local church, your kitchen, the park where you take your after-dinner walk, your shower—literally any place that feels comfortable. Your ritual could be daily, monthly, or yearly, depending on what you feel you need. I remember one older couple who remarried, each having been widowed after fifty years of marriage. Every morning they rose and lit a candle as a way of recognizing that the spirits of their deceased partners were "in" the new relationship, to acknowledge the past, and to help them celebrate the new life they both were experiencing.

Start a new ritual of remembrance by recognizing a characteristic or loving memory of your deceased loved one. If there are certain memories with special meanings you want to recall—a favorite meal, a special place, or a past experience—weave them into your ritual. Whatever you choose, dedicate yourself to incorporating it into your life. Whatever you decide on will not only provide order and direction and nourish you while you mourn, it will also help you establish a healthy new relationship with the deceased. Rituals truly illustrate the notion that what you focus on expands.

Here's one more lightening-quick yardstick to evaluate your progress in expanding a positive and eliminating a negative at any given moment. Ask yourself one question: *Right now, am I focusing on what's good, what's right, or am I focusing on what's not good, what's not right for me?* You should be primarily focusing on the present moment, not on the future or the past. Giving your full attention to living in the present—one day at a time—is one of the paths back to joy. Follow Andrew Carnegie's advice for reducing worry: "Live in day-tight compartments."

Remember, the most important steps are the steps that you take in your mind. Whenever you start doubting, whenever you feel that you're lagging behind in your grief work, whenever you see a couple or a family that reminds you of your loss, use that moment as an immediate springboard for reviewing:

- All the legacies from your loved one you will forever possess.

- The simple pleasures in your life that cost nothing to enjoy.

- All of the priceless relationships that are still yours, including the one with your beloved. Remember, that relationship is forever ongoing!

ADJUSTING YOUR EXPECTATIONS FOR GRIEF

Part of the reason negative thoughts can have such an influence on grief is because of the low expectations we've created for the process of grieving itself. On top of the profound sadness we inevitably face after the loss of a loved one is the deeply ingrained expectation—both in our own hearts and in others—that we should be devastated by that loss. But it doesn't have to be that way. If you can take a step back from yourself and raise your personal expectations for dealing with loss, you will be better able to make it through the massive change in your life.

Remember, *what you expect invariably changes what you experience.* If you can habitually focus your attention on the positive power of the unseen (the same power expressed in Extraordinary Encounters), you will see changes in your life. The key word here is *habitually*: You must ingrain a new habit. Make it an automatic response to replace the old restraining expectations about life with a belief in the good things that can and will prevail.

It's important to remember that your past does not determine your future. Freud had it wrong! You're not locked into the way you experience the present or the way you respond to loss. You are not a victim of circumstances, insensitive parents, or implacable genes. Don't let yourself fall into that pattern of thought—because there are few thoughts more destructive than that the death of your loved one prevents you from having a good future. All loss experiences are transient; life will get better, if you allow it to.

Remember, what you're really doing in the mourning process is starting a new life, in effect building a new identity and way of living without the physical presence of your loved one. Don't deny the fact that life has changed irrevocably; instead, work on accepting the reality of your changed world, the new duties and the obligations it implies. Honor the past, but don't hold on to it too tightly. You're not forgetting your old life or your loved one; you're simply moving into the next chapter of life. *What you focus on expands.*

The responsibility to create this new meaning is yours. Don't settle for merely getting by—grow from the experience of loss. You are a new you. When you look back at the past and events you experienced, learn from the mistakes that you (or other people) made. A parent or friend who said the wrong thing, or was abusive or ambivalent to you in your time of need, can teach you the importance of forgiveness, love, and commitment if you only choose to look past the hurt. Your goal is to take only wisdom from the past and apply it to your new life. You just have to believe that you always have the power to change.

CONNECTIONS BRING HEALING

Why is it so important to think openly about what happened to you in the past? Because of the past's connection to emotional repression, depression, and chronic anger, the results of separation, isolation, and perceived mistreatment. The less you are able to let go of traumatic events in your past, the longer you will spend grieving, and the more you will find yourself isolated from the people around you. If you let yourself believe that you'll never get a break; that you can't deal with the loss or change you are facing; that you won't be able to pay the mortgage or get the job you need; you'll find even more obstacles in your path. That kind of negative thinking causes you to shut down, to narrow your outlook on life. When you keep your thoughts on what you don't want—whether it's an emotion like fear or continued loneliness—you attract more of the same. Conversely, hope and love, which spring from feelings of connectedness to others, have long been proven to be health-promoting.

Take special note of what I just said: *Being connected to others is at the heart of coping well with your loss.* And I do mean "others." You need more than one good relationship to cope well with loss—you may even need a support group. Interconnectedness is the counterbalance to the unwelcome changes we all have to face, and friendship is a very staple of life. Failure to cultivate these connections will rob you of emotional strength and breed fear, paralyzing your ability to heal effectively. It's never too late to cultivate relationships with the people around you, people who are responsible and uplifting. Look around you at the people who seem to always have a smile on their face (incidentally, smiling is a proven immune system booster). Examine the way they deal with problems connected with loss, laugh at themselves, and appreciate the people in their lives. Notice how they make love a central part of their thoughts and appreciate what they have.

Make a list of people with whom you've lost touch, and make an attempt to contact them. Visualize peacefulness, friendship, joy; make those feelings a priority in your thoughts and actions. Most important, ask yourself this question: *In coping with the death of my loved one, do I live each day how I know he or she would want me to carry on?*

As we've explored, the art of staying positive in the midst of loss and change is a lifelong challenge. Loss can be such an unrelenting factor in life; it's easy to slip into depressive thinking. But I'm here to tell you that you can reawaken the joy inside you, and obliterate the emptiness you feel deep within. How? By being determined to develop your ability to refocus your attention, to change emotional gears when change is needed most. All it takes is determination, as this part of the poem *Will*, by Ella Wheeler Wilcox, suggests:

> *There is no chance, no destiny, no fate*
> *that can circumvent or hinder or control*
> *the firm resolve of a determined soul.*

Say it to yourself again and again, especially when things are not going as you had hoped. Keep coaching yourself, knowing that the determining factor in coping well is what you *think* you can do.

In the following chapter I challenge the common, fear-driven thought that pervades many loss experiences: that you're all alone in facing the future. Nothing could be farther from the truth. Everyone who has experienced an EE can attest to the dramatic evidence that we are never alone in our sorrows.

❧

Obstacles cannot crush me, every obstacle
yields to stern resolve. He who is fixed to a star
does not change his mind.

—LEONARDO DA VINCI

CHAPTER FOUR

WE ARE NOT ALONE

My religion consists of a humble admiration of the illimitable superior spirit who reveals himself in the slight details we are able to perceive with our frail and feeble minds. That deeply emotional conviction of the presence of a superior reasoning power, which is revealed in the incomprehensible universe, forms my idea of God.

—ALBERT EINSTEIN

Who or what is responsible for all of the life-changing moments—those synchronistic occurrences that we know couldn't just be coincidences—that take place millions of times every day throughout the world? Some people, like Eric Zalas, whose story you're about to read, are sure they know the answer. After Eric's wife died unexpectedly, he had an experience that led him to the conclusion that someone is always looking out for us. He came to believe, as I do, that we are never alone.

November 28, 2001—Thanksgiving weekend, normally a time for family, good food, and good times, had been dreadful. My wife, Jacquelyn, my sweetheart for the past twenty years, had died suddenly in her sleep from a rare viral attack only a month earlier. I found her early one Saturday morning. She had collapsed onto the bedroom floor sometime during the night. It is such a horrible shock to find the love of your life dead. I was alone now and grief-stricken by her loss. All I could do for the past four weeks was cry and continuously ask God why this had to happen to me.

My wife and I were in the process of selling our beautiful home in Illinois to move to Wisconsin, where I had started a new job just a few months earlier. During this transition period, I would spend my weekends with Jacquelyn and then make the three-hour drive up to Wisconsin first thing on Monday mornings. My new employer was putting me up at a hotel near the office until the sale of our home in Illinois closed.

It was the middle of the week after Thanksgiving and I had just finished my last meeting of the day around five-thirty in the afternoon. I was exhausted from my day's work and all the emotional stress of Jacquelyn's death. My mind started to wander, and I reflected that it would be nice to be home right now. At that instant the image of my hotel room came into my mind. I immediately broke down and began to cry. I felt so pathetic. What had happened to my life? The love of my life was gone and my idea of home had turned into a hotel room. My life had clearly hit rock bottom. It was almost too much for my spirit to bear.

I tearfully left the office and decided to go out and do some shopping to relax. After wandering around the local mall for an hour, I decided to head back to my hotel room. My room, actually a small suite, was on the third floor of the hotel. As I exited the elevator, I began walking toward the end of the hallway. At that moment I noticed a room ahead of me to my right that had a wonderful Christmas wreath decorated with little ornaments hanging on the door and an inviting floor mat outside. How charming, I thought to myself. Somebody really wants to make their hotel room feel like home. I had traveled extensively around the country for business, but never before had I ever seen somebody decorate the outside of their hotel room in this fashion. While striding past the door, I wondered what the person who was staying in the room was like. I turned the corner and continued heading toward my suite.

After taking a few steps I heard a door open in the hallway behind me and to my left. For some reason I stopped in my tracks and looked backward, over my shoulder. I was tired, hungry, and emotionally drained, yet something made me walk back to the end of the hallway and look to see who was there. Upon reflection, this was very strange because I didn't know any of the other guests at the hotel. When I reached the end of the hall, I saw a middle-aged woman leaving the room with the fancy wreath on the door. She was average height with blond hair and was wearing dark pants, a red sweater, and a white turtleneck. She was holding a small white poodle in her arms. I'm a bit ashamed to admit that the first thought that came to mind was that I hate poodles. Nevertheless, I smiled and said, "So you're the person who's staying in the room with the floor mat and wreath. I noticed them today and reflected how wonderful it is for you to decorate the outside of your hotel room in that way. Your room entrance really looks nice." The woman immediately thanked me with a big smile and approached me like we were old friends. She then said her name was Pam and introduced me to her poodle, Chloe. Pam explained that her husband, Larry had just accepted a new job in the area, and she wanted to give their hotel suite a special feeling for the holidays. Then Pam asked me if I was married.

At that instant I just lost my composure. Words

wouldn't form. My shoulders slumped and the roof of my mouth started to ache. Tears began to fall from my eyes. I sobbed openly. Between deep breaths, I stammered out that my wife had just died suddenly in her sleep last month and that my life was a mess. Pam put her arm around me and began to comfort me in the hallway. She immediately led me through the door back into her hotel suite and asked me to tell her what happened. I stood next to a long end table and began sharing my story with Pam. I told her how Jacquelyn and I had spent a romantic weekend just before she died, dancing, kissing, and being very much in love. She was so vibrant that weekend. Then she became sick the following Friday. We both thought it was the flu, so I cared for her that evening and put her to bed. I was sobbing uncontrollably as I told Pam how Jacquelyn never woke up that next morning. I had never been able to cry during my entire adult life, but now tears were streaming down my face, wetting my shirt, and actually forming pools on the table. Pam kept her arms around me and hugged me while I cried.

Pam sat me down in a plush chair and asked me if I would like a cup of hot tea. It sounded wonderful, and I nodded my approval while wiping the tears from my eyes. As she made the tea in the small kitchen area, I began to notice the furnishings in the suite. Their furniture was different from my suite, very nice actually. There was a wonderful Persian rug in the living area and matching large, overstuffed chairs and sofa in a beige fabric. Even the end tables and lamps were different. I mentioned this to Pam, and she explained that they wanted to make their stay comfortable, so they removed the hotel furniture and brought in their own things. How marvelous, I thought. While sipping on my tea, I noticed that the walls were covered with paintings of angels in large, golden frames. Some were Renaissance style, like Raphael's angels, while others were based on more modern interpretations. Between some of the paintings were ceramic or stone angel wall ornaments. I observed that many of them looked like cherubs. There was even a small statue of an angel on the table next to my chair.

We continued to talk for hours. Pam's voice was so comforting to me. She was saying all the right things. My spirit was being uplifted by her sympathetic and encouraging words. Then the door to the suite suddenly opened and a man entered. At that instant I felt embarrassed and a bit uneasy, thinking this must be Pam's husband. Imagine coming into your hotel room late at night to find a strange man in the room talking with *your wife. Yet when Larry entered the room and saw me, he showed absolutely no facial expressions or body language that suggested any hint of surprise or distress. Pam introduced me and immediately told Larry about my loss. He walked up to me and put his hands on my shoulders and said how sorry he was to hear about the death of my wife. Larry was about average height and build, with short, dark hair and an engaging smile. He sat next to Pam on the sofa and we chatted for another thirty minutes. During our conversation, Larry said that I was now at the start of a spiritual journey and that with the help of God, the Holy Spirit, and special angels, I would succeed. I was getting tired and a little hungry, so I thanked Pam and Larry for their kindness and got up to leave. They both gave me a big hug and said good night. As the door closed, I looked more closely at the Christmas wreath on the door to their suite and noticed that it was decorated with little golden angels.*

When I came home from the office the following day, I walked past Pam and Larry's room and noticed that the Christmas wreath and floor mat were gone. I knocked on the door but nobody answered. After dinner that night I walked downstairs and talked to the night manager at the hotel. I asked if I could get the name and address of the couple in Suite 314 that checked out that morning because I wanted to send them a small gift of gratitude for their kindness. The night manager checked on the computer and then said that nobody had been in Suite 314 the entire week. I said that there must be some mistake because I was in their suite last night. She rechecked her screen and then suggested that I must have the wrong room number.

I was stunned. Yet, as I walked back to my room, I knew what I saw and what I had experienced. It was real. As the weeks passed by, I began to wonder if all the pictures and statues of angels in Pam and Larry's room were part of some celestial joke being played on me. Would I be able to figure out what was really happening? Now, twenty months later, I believe that Pam and Larry were my special angels sent to help me during my darkest hour after the death of my sweetheart. Their comfort and kindness lifted me from the depths of despair and put me on the road to enlightenment and discovery. I am a different man now after moving through the painful and difficult process of spiritual rebirth. I realize that none of us are alone because special angels are there to help us when difficult life lessons cause us to temporarily stumble off our path.

—Eric Zalas, Appleton, Wisconsin

You can see just how deeply Eric was affected by the experience—it actually brought a halt to his downward spiral of grief. The Extraordinary Encounter opened his heart to the peace and reassurance flooding his consciousness, the message that all is well. He realized there were angels there to comfort him. He was not alone.

You are not alone.

It would be a serious mistake to underestimate the power of Extraordinary Encounters of all kinds—from the most elaborate vision to the seemingly most inconsequential chance occurrence—to change our lives. Why? Because everything happens for a reason, even minor coincidences. In fact, life is completely permeated with meaningful coincidences, for reasons we shall soon explore. What I want to suggest to you is this: Coincidences are therapeutic, an unbreakable link between the soul and the superior workings of the universe.

Just read this letter from a woman in England named Donna.

I feel I must let you know how I happened upon your book, Messages and Miracles. *I was sitting in my mother's garden a week ago Sunday, 10 August 2003. I was discussing with my partner how I wish that I could have the positive attitude that my oldest brother has about there being life after life. My youngest brother, Mark, had passed away over a year ago, and even though there have been several incidents that other family members (and myself) are sure were contacts from him, I still needed more convincing. I was saying to my partner that there was only one real way to be sure, and that would be in my own passing.*

A few hours later I decided to go on the Internet to look for books that explain dreams. Mark has featured heavily in many of mine since his death. I came across a book that I thought might enlighten me. It was something like 10,000 Dream Symbols Explained, *and I proceeded to put it in the basket, and then followed the directions to check out. Low and behold, when I got to the checkout the total came to fourteen pounds, which I knew couldn't be correct because the book price was only eight pounds. When I looked at the order details, another book had found its way into my basket. I was about to delete the item, but when I read what the book was about—I could not believe it. It was your book,* Messages and Miracles, *and it listed everything in it that I had mentioned earlier that day in the garden to my partner.*

I am afraid to say that I had never seen nor heard of it or you, for which I apologize. I kept trying to retrace my history on the browser, and at no time had I viewed your book. It was under a different subsection, not connected with dreams. So I knew that my brother Mark was now getting very peeved at me and was probably saying, "How many times do I have to prove to her that I am still here!"

I do believe there is no other way to explain all of the things that have happened since Mark's death, except to say that these events must be after-death communications. Mark obviously wanted me to read the book because he was probably fed up with all the time he has spent around me trying to convince me that there is an afterlife. It's especially weird, because he did not believe in one when he was alive in physical form. But I know he would have gone out of his way to prove it to me.

—Donna Doyle, Tottenham, London, England

The vision that Eric had, Donna's seeming computer glitch—they don't seem to have much in common. But that's exactly my point. There's no one size or shape of Extraordinary Encounters. In both Eric's and Donna's stories, the deceased or a Higher Power did something to let the loved one know that he or she was not alone, that someone was out there for him or her, trying to get his or her attention. And in both cases the unexpected blessing redirected the way the living loved one walks in the world. No matter how big or small the moment or coincidence, if you open yourself to it, if you believe in the power of the universe behind it, if you accept the idea that you are not alone in your grief, you will find that your life can change for the better.

Extraordinary Encounters illustrate the fact that the unpredictable leads to the new. When you accept the mystery of coincidence, you open yourself to a budding sense of energy and aliveness, creating new options and possibilities to do things that were previously beyond your awareness. When you accept that the visions, dreams, and vast number of coincidences in your life are all part of an ordered plan in which we're offered the opportunity to discover and develop insight into our purposes, talents, and who we can become, you allow the universe to move you toward greater oneness with those around you, while increasing self-awareness, and inner growth. Really, what EEs do is to offer mourners the chance to follow a higher path, to view life through a new filter, to embrace ideas that add beauty to existence—to recreate a life filled with meaning. Because you *are* capable of building an equally meaningful life, despite the loss of your loved one, with the help of your Extraordinary Encounters.

Remember, as Jesuit philosopher and anthropologist Teilhard de Chardin reminds us, "We are not human beings having a spiritual experience, we are spiritual beings having a human experience." In other words, we cannot underestimate the importance of our spiritual health. And that's why we have to be open, as Eric and Donna were, to experiences that are spiritually significant, experiences that can change lives in profound ways.

COMING TO TERMS WITH SPIRITUAL POWER

Let's say we do "open ourselves" to spiritual experiences. What implications, if any, does that have for our relationship with organized belief systems? With formal religion? With the sciences? What does it mean to accept a Higher Power? What tenets are we accepting when we say that everything and everyone is interconnected?

The organizing power that connects life and the universe—believed in by 95 percent of Americans—has been given various names: God, Yahweh, Allah, the Absolute, the Goddess, the Universe, the Supreme Reality, Brahman, the Universal Source, the Tao, the Great Spirit, the Alpha and Omega, the More, the Higher Power. In my opinion, every name falls far short of adequately describing this intelligence. As you read on, insert your preferred name wherever I use one of the above. The point is only this: Whatever you call it, you accept the power in your life. *Life does have meaning. The Higher Power of the universe is constant, is loving, and can be a very concrete, positive influence in your life.*

A few months ago an older woman in my community was making her way to church, as she did each morning, to attend the 8 o'clock service. As she was crossing the street, she was hit by a van and was instantly killed. This woman had been married for fifty-six years. Needless to say, her husband and family were stunned and devastated by her sudden death. But the very next morning her husband and children were in the same church the woman had attended. They were praying—for the young man who had been driving the van. Two days later, at the funeral, they hugged and forgave him.

We've already talked about the importance and the power of forgiveness in the grieving process, in terms of creating a positive mindset. But now we can truly understand where that power comes from. The story I just told demonstrates that the power to forgive and pray for a person who has caused you a tremendous amount of pain comes directly from your belief in a loving Higher Power, and the realization that we are all connected to one another. The universe includes and incorporates us all in a web of love and caring. You are never alone or without guidance, if you are open to it and look for it. The power is always there, especially in the worst of times.

I want to go back to the idea of coincidence. As I've said throughout this book, the ability to recognize and accept unexplainable events—events that deviate from rational reality—is an important first step in understanding the wisdom inherent to the universe. That's where the phenomenon of coincidence or synchronicity comes in . . . with the right mindset, we can come to understand coincidences as signposts in the universe's plan, demonstrations of the invisible assistance it provides. These everyday epiphanies are truly valuable resources for coping with loss and adapting to continuous change. Perhaps Deepak Chopra puts it best: "You never know when a coincidence will lead to the opportunity of a lifetime."

A CHRONICLE OF COINCIDENCES

Like most phenomena, there are degrees of coincidence, ranging from the simple to the highly complex and hard to explain. Often, we are not consciously aware of the multiplicity of coincidences that impact our lives. But sometimes, the experience is just too incredible to miss—something that just screams out the refrain "Everything happens for a reason." Take this series of coincidences, first reported in *Life* magazine in 1950, as an example.

On March 1, fifteen members of a choir were due to meet at their church in the small town of Beatrice, Nebraska, at 7:20 P.M. for an evening of rehearsal. But for one reason or another, all fifteen members of the choir were late. One person's car wouldn't start, another had to finish her homework, the minister and his family were finishing up the week's laundry, a mother and daughter were late because the daughter was slow in waking up from a nap; every choir member had some kind of reason for not being on time.

At 7:25 P.M., an explosion caused by an undetected defect in the heating system obliterated the church building.

According to a mathematician who later studied the event, the chances of all fifteen people being late on that specific evening were somewhere in the realm of one in a billion. Idle coincidence? Or the universe stepping in and taking the reins?

A nurse I know had the following experience:

I need to share my experience about someone not *wanting you present at death. My mom and I talked a lot about death. She told me she didn't want me there when she died. I was hurt, but she explained why she felt that way—it was because of our closeness. She felt it would be too painful for me.*

The night before the morning she died, my car just wouldn't start. I couldn't get down to be with my mom! It ended up being the fuel injector, but I'm convinced— she broke my car! She knew it would be the only way I wouldn't be there.

I want to share just one more story before we go on. This one comes from a gentleman named I. D. Cramer in London.

Sometime in the middle of last year my daughter came to see me and told me that she felt that she could not continue to live with her husband and wanted a divorce. I tried to dissuade her from this course of action on that occasion and also on a few other occasions when she visited me, since she had only been married for three years and there were two children from the marriage. I was very disturbed and worried about what would happen. I wondered if they would be able to sort things out and remain together or whether they would split up. This was a time at which I missed my wife, Greta, more than ever, since my daughter was our only child. I felt very lonely because I had no one with whom I could discuss this problem as I would have with my wife had she been alive. One day I went downstairs with the intention of playing the piano. I sat down on the piano stool, looked at the picture of my wife, and then at my daughter's wedding photograph. I then addressed my wife's picture and said, "What is going to happen to Gina's marriage?" (Gina being the name of our daughter.) I had only just finished asking the question when my daughter's wedding photo fell flat on its face. I sat staring open-mouthed at my wife's photo—it seemed to me that my wife had answered my question and said, "It's over." A few days after that, my son-in-law rang to tell me he and my daughter were splitting up and that he had moved out of the house.

I hope the examples I've given you have proven how profoundly coincidence can affect people's lives. No matter how big or small, coincidences can be truly transforming—they can allow people to see themselves, their own lives, and the lives of the people around them, in a new light. My hope is that, after reading this book, you'll let coincidence be an agent for broadening your perspective on the meaning of life and loss, a means of tapping into the unexplained events in your life, which are a part of the spiritual universe in which you exist. Most of all, I hope you start letting coincidence demonstrate one very important fact, the fact I've mentioned again and again in this chapter: *You are not alone.*

STRENGTHENING YOUR BELIEF IN CONNECTEDNESS

As I've said, opening yourself to and accepting coincidence is one of the most important steps you can take when you're trying to solidify your belief that you're not alone in the universe. But there are a few other concepts that can help you along the way.

1. Say "hello" to your deceased loved one, not goodbye. Of all the misconceptions associated with the grief process, none is more damaging than the idea that mourners must let go of the deceased and "find closure" (where closure means the lack of a substantial relationship). Nothing could be farther from the truth. If you are actively grieving the death of a loved one, you don't have to work toward saying goodbye—as I've said before, death is a doorway, not a wall. People die, relationships do not. Love lives on. You have to move forward, but you don't have to forget. You can say "hello" to the person and everything he or she represented, paying tribute and celebrating his or her life and wisdom, carrying on his or her legacy in any number of ways.

Think of what your loved one saw in you, inspired in you. What characteristics have you developed because of the relationship you had? These are things you might have forgotten in the turmoil of your grief. In quiet moments dwell on the fact that your loved one is always walking the paths within your heart. If you feel the need, go ahead and talk to him or her! Say whatever you're thinking, feeling, or wondering out loud. I believe conversations with deceased loved ones should include questioning, disagreeing as well as agreeing. In the end you'll have the wisdom you need to make the right decision.

There will be some people in your circle of friends, as well as some therapists, who will tell you that holding on to a relationship with the deceased will have a negative impact on your life. There is some truth to what they say; sometimes, holding on *too* tight to the past prevents us from rebuilding our lives in the present. However, as long as you abide by the following guidelines, I'm confident your relationship with the deceased will be only a positive force.

- When it comes to making a decision, your judgment for what is best for you at the particular time must prevail. It might be useful to consider what the deceased would have done in a given situation, or recall a conversation you had about the topic (as I said, feel free to ask him or her a question and see what answer comes into your mind!). But you alone make final decisions in matters affecting your new life.

- You fully accept, both intellectually and emotionally, that the loved one is dead. The life he or she lived will always be remembered, yet you realize the loved one will not be returning in physical form.

- You believe and accept that you must build a *new and different* life without your loved one and reinvest your emotional energy in it.

2. Do the "write" thing. Keep a log of your everyday miracles. Write down the so-called synchronicities or coincidences that occur in your life, and think about them in a new and different light. Ask yourself, what is the message here? What is the significance of this event? Dwell on hidden meaning. When you actively look for the encouraging synchronicities in your life, you will discover more of their guiding lights. Your writing will help express your deep feelings about these events and point to actions you can take.

It's also important to keep a record of how these gifts specifically impact your life—the pieces of wisdom you get at just the right time, the circumstances that shape a much needed positive experience, the flashing insight you receive that helps solve a problem. They are reminders that someone loves you, that you are never truly alone. Get in the habit of giving thanks when they occur.

3. Read! People throughout the ages have pondered the Intelligence behind everything we see on earth. They represent the collective wisdom of centuries of thinking. Read the words written by the great names of history. Start with *The Book of Positive Quotations*, compiled and arranged by John Cook, and see what Paul Tillich, William James, Albert Einstein, John Greenleaf Whittier, James Russell Lowell, and many others have said about the universe. Contemplate this quote by a most respected scientist, Sir James Jeans: "The universe begins to look more like a great thought than a great machine." Or this one by Sir John Eccles, who won the Nobel Prize for Medicine in 1963: "I believe there is a fundamental mystery in my existence, transcending any biological account of the development of my body (including my brain) with its genetic inheritance and its evolutionary origin." Read and reread this powerful statement, one of my favorites, from the great mathematician and humanitarian, Albert Einstein: "The probability of life originating by accident is comparable to the probability of the unabridged dictionary resulting from an explosion in a print shop." Ponder what Max Planck, the Nobel Prize–winning physicist, more recently said in his acceptance speech for his work on the atom: "All matter originates and exists only by virtue of a force. . . . We must assume behind this force the existence of a conscious and intelligent mind. This mind is the matrix of all matter."

I would be remiss if I did not mention the work of Dr. Gary E. Schwartz at the University of Arizona. No one has taken a more scientific approach to studying a certain kind of unusual experience: the abilities of psychics to make contact with deceased loved ones. In his book, *The Afterlife Experiments*, he provides an array of compelling scientific evidence that human consciousness survives bodily death, in what he refers to as the living soul hypothesis. *The Afterlife Experiments* is a must-read for anyone who has the least bit of doubt that we are not alone. Let me emphasize that I am not in any way recommending that you visit a psychic medium; I'm only suggesting that you avail yourself of some of the powerful evidence for the existence of the invisible world of the spirit.

4. **Learn to trust mystery and the unseen.** In my many years as a counselor, I've had the opportunity to see how often the wisdom of mystery reduces the intensity of grief. As you're dealing with your loss, resist the tendency to deny that which cannot be understood. Trust in mystery and the unseen; let your faith in the eternal connection between the known and the unknown be your guide. Believe that the universe is on your side, is always available to guide and give refuge, and is constantly reaching out to help you. Talk to the universe! Reach out with your words, thoughts, and prayers, and the universe will respond.

I want to take a moment to talk more about prayer. I'll start by sharing another story. Several years ago, when I was living in a small community on Long Island, I had an unusual conversation with my personal physician, who was a native of India and had been practicing internal medicine in the United States for many years. "You have a very stressful occupation," I said. "How do you deal with your stress?" He paused for a moment. When he spoke, I was taken back by his candor. "I pray," he said. "Every day, I pray. I am a Hindu. I pray for success. Not monetary success," he emphasized. "I pray for the wisdom to make the right choices when I am with my patients. I also talk to them and tell them what I honestly think. Then I don't take my stresses home with me.

"You know," he continued, "my mother prayed for me to become a doctor. And here I am. Prayer is very important."

I was amazed at how open this unassuming physician had been with me. Clearly, prayer was a part of his way of life. This link he had established with his Higher Power was something he relied on for strength and guidance, day in and day out. Why do I mention this story here? Well, often counselors, psychiatrists, and caregivers are reluctant to talk or write about prayer as an intervention strategy. But time and time again, I've heard mourners tell me how much prayer helped them through their deepest periods of grief. Between those stories, the 80–90 percent of Americans who say they pray every day for a variety of reasons, and the studies that have proven that prayer does, in fact, have a positive effect on healing, I'm convinced: Prayer really works.

There's no single way to pray. If you don't believe in a

theistic God, you can pray to the broader Universe. Or you can simply pray to Nature. I once had a man in a support group who was mourning the loss of his wife. He had carried out her wish to be cremated and her ashes sprinkled in the Gulf of Mexico. "My wife was buried in the Gulf," he said. "Now I walk out on to the jetty and say a prayer for her. It makes me feel better." By connecting to the unseen world around them, mourners like that man can draw on spiritual energy to help them find peace and endurance, and to rebuild their lives—in other words, to do their grief work.

One method of prayer you might try is prayerwalking: literally, praying when you're out for a walk. As you're outside, communing with nature, hold a conversation with your Higher Power, your deceased loved one, or both. (Many people like to do this early in the morning.) Say the words of a prayer as you take your steps. To illustrate: Take a step for each of the following words, as you repeat these phrases: "All Loving Presence, help me to see your will" or "All Loving Presence, help me make the right decision." Notice the rhythm of your voice in relation to the rhythm of your steps. Make up your own prayers, or use others you believe to be more appropriate for your prayerwalking. Keep in mind the observation of Danish philosopher Søren Kierkegaard: "The right kind of prayer will widen your circle. Prayer does not change God, but it changes him who prays."

The right kind of prayer is sincere prayer. And I'm confident that sincere prayer will change the way you feel, providing you with a palpable sense of relief and comfort. It will help you remember that you are never alone.

5. Start a daily spiritual practice. I promise, it will recharge your spiritual energy and become a major force in your healing process. That practice could be the prayerwalking we just discussed, or it could be something entirely different. Take this story as an example: Navy Captain Gerald L. Coffee was shot down on a reconnaissance mission over North Vietnam after having taken off from an aircraft carrier, the U.S.S. *Kitty Hawk*. Finally reaching Hanoi, he was thrown into a cell where the first two English words he saw scratched on his cell wall were God=Strength. "It worked for me," he said. "Every prisoner there had a daily spiritual routine." Coffee should know. He was imprisoned for seven years and nine days.

I can't stress this enough: A daily spiritual practice, whether meditating, writing, chanting, expressing gratitude—whatever is right for you—is an essential part of navigating the grief process. It will help you learn that you are never alone, because it constantly puts you in contact with the vibrant, loving universe around you.

6. If you need something, ask for it. I tell every client who comes to me that there is nothing wrong with asking or praying for a sign that your loved one is okay. You will receive a sign when you need it most. Be patient. Persist. Be specific. Keep petitioning. Stay alert and increase your awareness of the coincidences, feelings, unusual happenings, intuitions, and good things that occur during your day. Give thanks when what you have prayed for arrives. Persistent prayer cannot be denied. In particular, ask your Higher Power to allow you to have a visitation dream. Many spiritual counselors believe that dreams are the easiest way for spirits to communicate with survivors.

You might also combine your prayers with meditation. If prayer is talking to the Intelligence, meditation is listening to that Intelligence. Meditation—opening your mind and heart to the messages of the universe around you— will put you in an ideal state of consciousness to receive an Extraordinary Encounter. One of the most common forms of meditation is simply sitting silently, in a comfortable position, and repeating the name of your Higher Power (Jesus, Allah, Yaweh, Lord of All) each time you slowly exhale a breath. Another powerful affirmative meditation, which can alleviate even your deepest feelings of isolation, involves saying the following: "I am an important person to (the name of your Higher Power) because I am a part of his/her creation and likeness." Say the words slowly; pay attention to the images you see in your mind. These images are points of contact with your loved one—signs that you are not alone!

You can also call on the meditative practices of Zen Buddhism, the Kabbalah, contemplative Christianity, or yoga, all of which expand consciousness and open up new territory in the world of spirit. Whatever you choose to do, remember to start slow, with a two-minute meditation. Then slowly start increasing your time. Twenty to thirty minutes should be your goal.

Finally, if something unusual happens to you during your prayer or meditation session, and you are not sure how to assess it, ask yourself four questions:

- Is this the kind of thing my loved one would do?

- What is my intuitive feeling about the event? (Notice what comes into your awareness—what thoughts, physical feelings, emotions.)

- Has this event brought the feeling that love has been given and received?

· Most important of all, did the experience bring peace?

If the answer to the last question is yes, you should feel confident that you're being led by a power greater than yourself, regardless of the name you attach to it. I firmly believe that peace and a sense of belonging or connectedness go hand in hand, and that the road to true healing lies in following that peace.

In closing this chapter, I want to share one more story, and one more lesson. It you ever find yourself slipping backward toward the old belief that you're all alone in the universe, just remember what happened to a woman named Patty. . . .

My father, Dr. Robert N. Wry, was a wonderful man, my personal hero. He was a chiropractor and a compassionate human being who cared for his patients, even the ones who could not afford his services. Dad was a handsome and fit man who did not look his age. He had just turned seventy on December 7, 2003. He had recently had a physical, and the doctor said he wished all his patients were as healthy. That is what makes his death even more tragic.

On January 4, 2004, just after dinner, he stood up from the table and walked over to the fireplace. Mom said she heard a funny noise, and when she looked over at him he was grimacing and his hands were shaking. He took two steps and went down. He was rushed to Port Angeles Hospital (we live in Sequim, Washington) and then flown to Virginia Mason in Seattle. He had encephalitis caused by the chicken pox virus. We were told it was very rare and that most people usually get shingles from it. He clung to life getting more weak and frail each day—but still fighting. Dad lost his battle January 27, 2004. To say we were devastated doesn't begin to cover it. We held him and told him we loved him, kissed him, and made sure he knew we were not mad at him for dying. We stayed there with him so he would not be alone.

I should note that my dad did not believe in life after death. I wanted to believe, but when the smartest man you know says its nonsense, it's hard to keep up hope.

Dad had a beautiful new Dodge 4x4 pickup. He loved that truck. It was the first really expensive toy he ever bought. After he died, Mom gave it to me. After a little while I tuned and set three of the radio stations to my favorite channels. Number 1 was good-time oldies, 2 was KMPS country, and 3 was classic rock. I left number 4 alone, as it was dad's favorite classical station. One day I was driving down the road listening to the

*country station when all of a sudden, I start hearing a
lot of talk—the radio was on Dad's classical station. I
thought I must have accidentally hit the button, so I
turned it back. Then again, I looked down and saw it
was on preset 4. I turned it back. Again, it switched to
4. This kept happening until I got too fed up and just
turned the radio down.*

*The next day, without thinking, I got into the truck,
turned up the volume, hit station 2. Not long after, it
switched back to station 4. After a few times of going
from 2 to 4, I turned the radio off and decided to ask
Mom if they had any problems with it. After all, it was
a new truck.*

*On day three my fiancé, Ric, and I took the truck to
Tacoma to visit Ric's mom. Ric likes good-time oldies, so
I put the radio on preset 1. A few minutes later it automatically turned to 4. I changed it back, but it did it
again. I told Ric how it had been doing that. While we
waited on the Hood Canal Bridge for a submarine to
go through, Ric put the radio on the first programmed
station, and we watched it change to 4. Ric then said,
"Bob, is that you? Knock it off. It's okay; we won't hurt
your truck." At that moment it hit me! I felt Dad. I felt
his exasperation at trying to get my attention—and his
relief that finally someone noticed it was him. My face*

got a really warm and fuzzy feeling like his hands were cupping it. I felt electricity running through my body and an internal knowledge that he was right there. I started to cry and said to him, "Dad if this means you're okay, then we'll be okay, too." I thanked him for his gift of contact. The radio changed from 1 to 4 after I said that. It has never again changed to 4 since that eventful day.

I wish I could have seen his face when he stepped out of his body and into his next life! I know that he had to contact me to let me know that he was wrong—life goes on. I know this more than anything I've ever known. I feel joy and pride that my dad is so smart, and kept at it until we got the message. It's just like him to protect me, even in death. This experience has changed my life and outlook on death forever.

The next chapter brings us to a core concept for dealing with *any* type of loss experience, one that every EE directly or indirectly points to: as mourners, our responsibility and need to adapt. Eventually almost every mourner comes to terms with one realization: that he or she has to change in some way.

May not such events {coincidences} raise the suggestion that they are not undesigned, and that Heaven does so order things, as sometimes to attract strongly the attention, and excite the thoughts of men?

—DANIEL WEBSTER

CHAPTER FIVE

ACTION HEALS

*A young woman once said to an old woman,
"What is life's heaviest burden?" And the old
woman said, "To have nothing to carry."*

—JEWISH PROVERB

*One of the best ways to change is to act as if you
are the person you want to become.*

—BERNIE SIEGEL, M.D., IN *PRESCRIPTIONS FOR LIVING*

Grieving isn't just about coming to terms with the events around you (including whatever Extraordinary Encounters you may have experienced). Healthy grieving also involves a highly personal element of growth and change. You can't just wait for solace to come and find you—you have to go out and get it. Remember, our departed loved ones don't want us to be so consumed with feelings of loss that our lives are permanently altered for the worse. They want us to move forward with our lives and our new relationships. Just take this EE as an example. . . .

I was very close to my grandfather my whole life. He was always there for me with encouragement and love. As a parent, my grandfather was very strict. My father and his brother and two sisters always knew that when their dad spoke, they listened. With me, it was so different— until he had to get firm with me after his death.

When I heard my grandfather had died, I was so overcome with grief, I cried as though my heart would break. At the time of his death, my son was only two years old, and I felt he was cheated in not getting to know my grandfather. I was absolutely consumed with grief, because even though my grandfather was eighty-two, he was a young eighty-two, and his death was very unexpected for me.

The day after the burial, I went back to the cemetery. It was a clear, cold, sunny day in Buffalo, New York, and the wind was very still. As I stood there crying about how much I missed my grandfather, the wind suddenly picked up and got very strong. The flowers on his grave shook. And then I heard very clearly, in a very strict, firm voice: "Go home and live!" It was so loud, I put my hands over my ears and turned to see who was behind me. There was no one. Again I heard: "Go home and live!" I admit at first that I was very, very scared. I even ran back to my car, my heart racing. As I got near my car, the wind started to die down, and I felt this very warm, loving, peaceful feeling come over me. My grief was lifted, and I felt acceptance of my grandfather's death. The message I have always believed I got that day was this: I love you, I always have, but you have things you need to do here, and I have things I need to do where I am. I will always be with you in spirit, but you need to go home and live your life.

—*Pam Lytle, Mason, Ohio*

TALK DOESN'T COOK RICE

When they're alive, our loved ones often show or teach us how to act when we are challenged by demanding choices in life. Pam's grandfather had done it many times before— and continued to do so in his visit to her at the cemetery. Death cannot take away our loved ones' power to give us direction and guidance.

When you think about it, all EEs leave behind one clear-cut message: The ball is in our court. They force us to ask ourselves: *What are we going to do now? What can we do differently in our lives? How will we use our loved one's inspiration to make a plan, take a new direction, and adapt to the conditions we currently face?* You've probably heard someone say, "You have to make it happen or it isn't going to happen." The Chinese put it much more succinctly: "Talk doesn't cook rice." In other words, what you actually *do* is one of the most important steps in the grieving process. Action and change are life-sustaining. Even the smallest steps can make a huge difference in your confidence and emotional stability.

It's a bit of a double-edged sword: Extraordinary Encounters indisputably encourage us to move on with our lives. However, some EE recipients fall into the trap of always looking for more—another gift, another visitation, more guidance or comfort. A couple of years ago, I was giving a talk in Cleveland, Ohio. A woman in the audience, we'll call her Janine, stood up and explained that she had had three or four Extraordinary Encounters after the death of her young son. They were helpful to her; she was convinced of their authenticity, and they were comforting. "But," she continued, "I want to see him just one more time." She failed to see that she had already been given ample opportunity to accept his death and the fact that his spirit lived on, and that she should have been starting the transition of living without the physical presence of her son.

What the woman needed to do was to start life anew, take on new roles and skills. She had to focus less on her son's physical absence and more on establishing a new relationship with him. In other words she had to really begin her grief work, or as psychotherapist and Harvard Professor J. William Worden would say, complete the four major tasks of mourning.

1. **Accept the reality of the loss.**

2. **Experience the pain of grief.**

3. **Adjust to an environment in which the deceased is missing.**

4. **Withdraw emotional energy and reinvest it in new rewarding relationships.**

I once heard a woman who had lost her seventeen-year-old son in a tragic automobile accident (and who later became a facilitator for a Compassionate Friends bereavement group) say, "Time doesn't heal all wounds unless you work between the minutes." What a wonderful quote. It demonstrates the fact that it takes action to heal, to deal with all of the emotions associated with grief, as well as the task of reconstructing a shattered life. You're not going to get better if you just sit around and wait for time to do the job. Remember, EEs are the way our loved ones communicate with us after they've passed on—the way they help us turn from sorrow and begin the climb back to life. But for your part, talk is cheap. Action is its own reward. Are you willing to adapt and move forward, or will you continue to live in the past?

TAKING THE FIRST STEP

The resolution to every problem you might face, regardless of its nature, begins with you. Pain—whether emotional, physical, or both—is a signal to take a new road in life. Take the first step, a different step. If it's something you'd rather not do, do it anyway. *Doing is surviving.*

I once knew a woman whose father had Alzheimer's disease. Even when he was already in his home, the father would constantly say, "Let's go home." Sometimes he would get belligerent. The whole situation was driving his daughter to her wits end. Then, she was given the following advice: When she'd had enough of her father's ranting, she was to respond to his wanting to leave by saying, "Okay, let's go." She was then to go outside with him, get into the car and drive around for a couple of minutes, and come right back home. It turned out the suggestion always worked, and helped her deal with a frustrating problem, even though most people would never have thought it worth a try. You'd be surprised how often trying the thing that seems most unusual or different is of the most help.

But sometimes the first step isn't that unusual or different. Sometimes it's something that is already a part of your life—something you don't have to reach that far to accomplish. Here are six simple, proven suggestions for initiating new habit patterns leading to a healthier you.

1. Do something physical. The next time the blues hit or you feel all alone, refuse to allow the thoughts to keep you inert and isolated. Change your immediate position or surroundings—step into the next room, do a chore, run outside to do an errand, or turn on the radio. (As one widower said, "Just get out of the house!") The movement could even be as simple as changing your physiology, the way you're sitting. Try it right now, it's easy. Wherever you are reading this book—whether it's on a bus, train, or in your favorite chair—immediately do the following: Make a note of your posture and also of the way you feel. Are you tense in any areas? Now, lift your head up, straighten your back, throw back your shoulders, and fold your hands, letting them rest on your lap. See how alert and ready you feel in comparison to when you were in your passive, slouched posture? You just changed your physiology, and presto, look what it did for your thoughts. Try the same thing when you're walking whenever possible. Walk tall and stretch your body upward. Lift your head, pull your shoulders back, and lift your chest as you take deep breaths. You can also try writing out what you are feeling (yes, writing counts as an action!) When you're finished doing whatever it is you did, you'll not only feel better emotionally, you'll have a sense of achievement, which will stop the downward spiral toward deeper depression.

2. Create a "but" list of responses. Imagine someone says to you, "It must be hard for you, being alone." How are you going to respond? Not with, "Yes, it is." You should respond with "Yes, *but* I'm creating some new interests" or "Yes, *but* I'll turn the corner on this." You don't have to deny the truth of your sadness, but you *do* have to focus on the ways you're working on improving the situation. To that end, make up a personal "but list" of responses. Read them to yourself. Believe in them. I promise, they'll help keep you in the right frame of mind to maintain your action plan, keep your hopes up, practice your faith, and affect the desired changes.

3. Develop a routine that reflects your goals. Helen Keller once said, "When one door of happiness closes, another opens; but often we look so long at the closed door that we do not see the one that has been opened to us." In other words, as mourners, we have to focus on new opportunities. But how do we actually put those opportunities into practice? By being habitual and consistent. For example, if you wish to strengthen a relationship with a family member, coworker, or friend, establish a consistent time you can get together with that person, just like this person did. . . .

As a young hospice volunteer, every Tuesday afternoon, I used to visit a man in the program who was dying of cancer. He counted on me being there at a specific time, as soon as I got out of work, and he looked forward to our visits. Whether raining or snowing, I made every effort to show up at the appointed time. My expected visits with him were a major reason for him saying to me one day, "You know, if it wasn't for you, I don't think I would be here now." I was stunned when he said that. Little did I realize that my Tuesday afternoon ritual of visiting, regardless of the elements, was instrumental in the close relationship we had developed. Consistency breeds trust and is the backbone of relationships and traditions that grow and become meaningful.

4. Start listening to your body. If your body could talk, what would it say about how you treat it, the fuel you give it, and the demands you make of it? Would it tell you to take a hike—either literally or figuratively? Or would it say, "Wake up, take care of me." For over forty years, I have taught that *for every thought and emotion we have, there is a corresponding physical manifestation of that thought or emotion in the body.* Research into the relationships between the central nervous system, endocrine system, gastrointestinal system, and immune system (called psychoneuroimmunology) bear this out. The body and mind do a lot of talking to each other—your thoughts can physically weaken you, or exacerbate whatever you are physically feeling. The stress of prolonged grief, especially guilt, anger, shame, and depression, compromises the ability of the immune system to combat hostile microorganisms. The proof? Many mourners come down with colds and flulike symptoms over time.

Here's just a quick demonstration of the body-mind relationship: Close your eyes for a moment and picture yourself holding a large, bright, yellow lemon. Notice the texture. Now see yourself taking a big bite into it. Feel the lemon juice in your mouth. What did you experience? A chill? Goose bumps? There you have it—your thoughts directly influenced your body.

But the good news is, there's a way to fight back. Positive thinking will unleash a barrage of hormones and chemicals helpful to the body, chemicals that can enhance your well-being and reduce the effects of stress. Even if you can't stop discouraging thoughts from suddenly popping up in your head, you can certainly decide not to accept them, and combat them with an assertive thought. If you can do that, your physiology will just go along for the ride.

The body-mind relationship is really a two-way street. As much as the mind influences the body, the body also heavily influences our thought processes. When we are ill, tired, or hungry, we often say and do things that seem out of character. We may be impolite, easily get angry, or make questionable decisions. Conversely, when we feel good, we're more open and willing to engage others, more sociable, and better able to fulfill our responsibilities. That's why it's so important to *rest* when you're grieving. Mourning is hard work—you have to allow yourself time to replenish. Get plenty of sleep, as difficult as that is; eat wisely by reducing your caffeine intake and adding water and a green salad to your diet. Be sure to exercise—walking is absolutely essential! Always remember, your loved one wants you to go on with a healthy and successful life!

5. Form a study group. Reach out to your circle of friends, your family, your church—whomever you choose—and form a study group to discuss common coping strategies for dealing with loss and change. Choose a specific loss— a separation, death, divorce, or geographical change, for instance. Take it upon yourself to gather some reading materials that address the issue, and share them with the group. Encourage everyone to contribute by suggesting that each group member take responsibility for leading a meeting and recommending reading materials. Loss and change are conditions we have to deal with for the duration of our existence. There are no exceptions.

6. Focus your thoughts. Remember what we talked about in Chapter 3? *What you focus on expands. What you continually expose yourself to will eventually shape the way you think, feel, and act.* For that reason, you have to be vigilant of the places you go, the things you read, the television shows you watch, the music you listen to, and the people you hang out with. Be aware of how these things influence your emotions: Do they encourage you to be passive, sad, listless, and constantly remind you of your painful loss? If

the answer is yes, those things are toxic, and you have a responsibility to put a stop to them.

Whatever step you choose to take—whether it's simply improving your posture, going for a walk, picking
up the phone, going to your study group—the key is
only that you act decisively. You've probably heard
someone say it before. I'm going to say it again: Procras-
tination is a thief that steals time, time you'll never get
back. It steals opportunities that could make a major
difference in the quality of your life. We have a limited
amount of time in life, and when we refuse to do what
we know we should do for whatever reason—being
scared, being uncomfortable, or just not feeling like it—
we only prolong the grieving process. Wherever you go,
carry this quote from Martin Luther King, Jr. with you:
"You don't have to see the whole staircase, just take the
first step."

SUSTAINING THE ACTION

Now, we've talked about taking the first step. It's never an
easy thing to do. But unfortunately, in some ways it's easier then what comes next. It's one thing to muster up the
initial courage to take action. However, what happens

when you encounter a roadblock or feel as though you're not making enough headway? Will you become discouraged and falter?

The most important thing about taking action is something that most of us never plan for: *sustaining it.*

So, how do you go about doing it? How can you keep yourself from becoming discouraged? How do you restart a stalled engine? The answer is, plenty of ways. Here are seven critical elements that will help keep you moving forward.

1. Set short-term goals. You *must* have a clear goal in mind. Set short-term goals (or a single goal early in your grief) for healing and growth. Make your survival plan clear and direct by deciding what is of immediate importance. For example: *I want to get through this day or hour. I want to walk by myself in the park. I want to think of my loved one without tearing up.* Make a daily task list that includes what you need to do. Be specific on what thoughts and actions you will employ, and how you will avoid the occasions when you dwell on unwanted emotions. Realize you can't prevent unwanted thoughts from suddenly popping into your head, but you can develop specific strategies, even one as simple as turning and walking in the opposite direction, to reduce their impact.

2. Develop *new* routines. I sat next to Sue, a young widow who had been in one of my support groups, in church one Saturday afternoon. The service started with a hymn. When it was finished, she turned to me and said, "I sang that this morning." I smiled and nodded. Midway through the service, another familiar hymn was sung and again, when it was finished, she turned and said, "I sang that this morning." I finally remarked, "You must have been here this morning for the early service." She turned and chuckled. "No, I was in the shower!" One of her new action routines, among others, was singing hymns when she showered each day to keep her spirits up.

Ask yourself: What new routines can you develop in your life? It could be eating at a different time, reading a book, exercising, taking your neighbor's dog for a walk—anything that helps bring normalcy and control back into life. On the other side of the coin, what can you do to stop falling back on the old routines that involved your loved one? Try to break away from that drink at five o'-clock, that daily trip to the grocery store, that walk in the evening—take it at a different time or place. It will be sad, at first, to let them go. They were a major part of your old life, and represent major secondary losses. But breaking them represents a huge step forward in the healing process.

3. Expect obstacles. Accepting change is seldom an easy transition because we like to hang on to our old predictable ways. You already know there is no quick fix or instant cure for grief. Implementing those new routines and adapting to any major change takes time and patience. It's a form of dying: We die to our old routines, our old life. And in many ways it's like learning a new language. You have to repeat and repeat the new words (new behaviors) or you forget them and revert to your native tongue. Just remember—there will always be challenges. There will always be good reasons to go back to your old routine, to revert to your native tongue. But you must stay strong in your course of action!

4. Use memories as motivation. This is a big key. When you're faced with setbacks, go back into your memory file and recreate the same visions and feelings that were your original inspiration. Put yourself in that same emotional frame of reference. Play those upbeat thoughts over and over again. And always remember this saying: "If at first you don't succeed, you're about average . . . and try, try again."

Remember, you have a remarkable capacity to choose what you want to think (more on that idea shortly . . .). You can create a specific thought or recall a certain memory specifically to deal with fear or sadness. Write your action plan down and read it aloud to yourself everyday. Lastly, be flexible—allow for mid-course corrections as you move forward in your grief. You don't want to lock yourself into unreasonable expectations.

5. Keep your eye on the goal. Or as Henry Ford put it, "Obstacles are those frightful things you see when you take your eyes off the goal." That's why reading your plan every day (and revising it as you see fit) is a must. Run the endgame scenario through your thoughts again and again. What will your final triumphant moment be like? See and feel yourself enjoying your victory. Doing so will help you learn to persist, and give you the tenacity you need to stick with your plan, even when it requires a little extra effort.

6. Take advantage of your friends and loved ones. Find someone you trust, with whom you can share your plight. Ask that person, "What would you do if you were in my place?" or "How do you think I am doing with my plan?" Let him or her help you monitor your progress as you're attempting to deal with big changes. Just be certain it is a person who can be honest, candid, and objective, one whose empathy—not necessarily sympathy—is obvious.

Because baring your soul to a friend, possibly sharing your lack of motivation, can certainly be humbling. But it just as easily can result in the very motivation you need to restart your journey. You might even try to find a "companion-in-grief" who is also mourning to regularly meet with and/or call when you need to talk. That way, both of you can agree to help each other in this way.

7. **Do your research.** For an extra boost, look into how other people handled a similar problem. Make reading their words and insights a regular part of your day. An example might be this quote from Mohandas K. Gandhi, India's great peacemaker: "Be the change you want to see in the world." Rephrase it to your liking: "Be the person you want to be." Many years ago I asked a man I was visiting, who was dying of lung cancer, how he dealt with bouts of depression during the course of a day. How was he able to overcome that roadblock? It turned out he had discovered, without being told, that refusing to be immobile or to dwell on his sadness could turn his feelings around. "I get up and go in the kitchen and do the dirty dishes or I go outside," he said.

Remember, when those discouraging thoughts emerge—don't wait. Immediately act out your plan for dealing with the situation. As I said earlier, start by taking one first step. As Mark Twain said, "The secret of getting ahead is getting started. The secret of getting started is breaking your complex, overwhelming tasks into small, manageable tasks, and then starting on the first one." Do a little every day to demonstrate your commitment to moving toward your goal. Because there is no such thing as luck in dealing with change. "*Luck* is a very good word," a sage once said, "if you put a *P* before it."

ACTING AS YOU WISH TO BE

William James, who many believe to be the father of modern psychology, had much to say about implementing new behavior. "If you are troubled with one kind of emotion and want to change it to a better one," he said, "live on the assumption that you already have the other kind of emotion you desire. Do this assiduously, cold-bloodedly, regardless of what your mind tells you and, in due time, you will have it." In other words, act as though you believe that emotion is already in your arsenal. *Act as you wish to be.*

If you want to be happy, act like a happy person. If you want to be positive, do positive things. If you want to manage a fear, face the fearful situation with courage and a plan—and move on it. Use your Extraordinary Encounters to push your existing feelings of fear and discomfort aside and *do* what appears to be initially insurmountable.

The famous singer Nat King Cole sang a song with these opening lines: "Pretend you're happy when you're blue. It isn't very hard to do." Easier said than done, of course—yet the principle behind the line is well founded. Change your thoughts and you'll change your emotions. Do you remember playing "Let's pretend" when you were a child? Think of how you acted out the part of the soldier, the pilot, the doctor; the way you stirred your imagination. By playing "Let's pretend" once again, you can tap into the natural ability you possess to use your mind to change your reality.

It's not childish nonsense, if that's what you're thinking. Don't think of it as deceiving yourself; think of it as setting the stage to achieve what you seek. Acting as if you are where you want to be draws you to a higher consciousness, a higher level of performance. Because of the way it changes your thinking (especially on an unconscious level where it really counts), eventually, acting will bring about the desired state in reality. Bottom line: Start living on the assumption that you are already where you want to be. Soon your inner attitude and thoughts will meld with your actions.

A related issue is the concept of diversion. You can help your quest to act as you wish to be by diverting your mind away from painful thoughts. I often tell the people who come to me for counseling the story of a woman who was in one of my support groups. Listen to her description of what she did when she found herself inundated with unwanted thoughts. "I go to my bathroom and stand in front of the toilet," she said. "Then I take my hand and drag it across my forehead as though I am pulling the unwanted thoughts out of my mind. With a sweeping movement, I throw them into the toilet and flush them down the drain. I abruptly turn, walk out of the bathroom, and immediately take up another task or go outside." With that simple act, the woman symbolically rid herself of her negative emotions, diverted her mind from grief, and opened a door to a new activity.

I recommend you choose a verbal cue to help divert your thinking when you recognize you're spending too much time dwelling on the negative. It can be any word or phrase: "not now," "leave," "buzz off," or "time to move." Remember, you empower a negative concept and allow it to rule your thinking by repeating it, dwelling on it. So use your cue to change your self-dialogue. You always have a choice as to how you think about things. No matter how terrible your situation might be, you can represent it in your mind in a way that empowers you to go on.

I want to acknowledge that the concept of diversion is sometimes hard for mourners to handle. *Isn't this a betrayal of my loved one's memory?* they ask. *Shouldn't I be confronting my grief head-on?* The answer to that question is yes—but diversion can help you by putting you in a more balanced, healthy overall mindset. There is nothing wrong with diverting your attention from your grief, taking a short or a long break from thinking about what you have lost. As a mourner, you have a right to self-care, to respite. In fact, it's necessary in order to avoid physical and mental exhaustion. Accept an invitation to dinner or to go to a concert. Take a spontaneous walk in the park. Make no mistake, eventually the pain will resurface—and it will eventually be resolved. But it will be resolved through experiencing it little by little. You have to look at your grief as though it is an endurance race. As long as you keep moving forward, you will get your second wind.

MASTERING YOUR EMOTIONS

Over my years as a grief counselor, I've determined that the difference between those who have severe, prolonged grief responses and those who don't—the difference between moving forward or stagnating in the face of loss—is consistantly trying to respond to the unfamiliar, adapting to the new environment despite the searing pain. The "haves" consistently did the difficult thing at the time it had to be done. The "have-nots" held back, chose inaction, and prolonged their process of transition. In short, they chose *not* to do the undesirable.

There's an old saying many mothers and fathers have taught their children: Actions speak louder than words. It's a simple yet significant piece of wisdom and it applies to managing your emotions. No matter what your situation, actually meeting your goals is important—that's the best way to assess your progress. But of equal importance, and constantly overlooked, is the forgotten piece of the puzzle, the secret element in the quest for peace and progress—understanding that feelings are not the cause of behavior. You are not beholden to your emotions! *What you think and do causes what you feel,* either good or bad. Emotions don't just appear; we think them into existence. Something we are thinking, something we have or have not accomplished, is behind the way we feel at any given time, not the other way around. It is the failure to act (and, of course, imprudent actions) that is the source of ongoing guilt, anger, and depression. And it is our thoughts and actions that can dissolve negative feelings or distrust, and boost self-esteem. You have the power to adapt to loss, if you can muster the self-discipline to begin the process.

Now that you've almost finished this chapter, promise yourself that you'll do one thing. Within thirty minutes of putting this book down, start thinking of one strategy to address the answer to this question: *What is the most pressing need in my life at this time?* Write the strategy down immediately, and start acting on it. Don't put it off until tomorrow or next week—if you start off procrastinating, you'll never get it done. Take that first and most crucial step! "Even if you're on the right track," said Will Rogers, "you'll get run over if you just sit there." So, go for it. Now! Change your conditioning by setting the new conditions of your life. Your actions will lead to healing.

Keep on going, and the chances are you will stumble on something, perhaps when you are least expecting it. I have never heard of anyone stumbling on something sitting down.

—CHARLES F. KETTERING, ENGINEER AND INVENTOR

Now you know how you can build up your ability to take action as a means of coping with loss. But there's

more to it than that. The ability to act is infinitely enhanced and directly dependant on the quality of your
inner life. You can strengthen your inner life by initially
recognizing that *every* thought either lifts you up or
breaks you down, as you will learn in the following
chapter.

CHAPTER SIX

REBUILD YOUR INNER LIFE

Most true happiness comes from one's inner life, from the disposition of the mind and soul. . . . It takes reflection and contemplation and self-discipline.

—W. L. SHIRER

Loss experiences, especially the death of a loved one, challenge the quality and direction of our inner lives. In fact, they can turn our emotional worlds completely upside down. But we do have weapons we can use to fight back: something to do, something to love, and something to hope for. Those three "somethings," each one its own journey that starts from within, are always ready to meet the challenges of change. That's why I am confident in saying that your inner life is the one resource you can always count on to lead you to healing.

And what do Extraordinary Encounters do, if not

force us to focus on the inner dialogue going on in our hearts and minds? To shift our focus from a physical to nonphysical reality? EEs highlight the fact that joy, happiness, and peace of mind are ultimately things that come from within us. You can learn to find that inner balance, to utilize certain coping skills to reduce anxiety and bring happiness back into your life. Just like Lisa was able to do. . . .

When my husband's grandmother Nana passed away, I was very distraught. I had felt very close to her and loved her dearly. She lived in the same town as we did, and she and I had become good friends when I went over to visit her and at family gatherings. Even though she was in her eighties and I was in my thirties, we giggled like school chums when we were together. We really had a "connection." I always enjoyed her sense of humor and her company so much.

When she died, I felt extremely sad, more than I ever expected I would. Even though I had faith in God, Jesus, and an afterlife, I found myself crying out to God for proof that she was okay, that she was still alive, somewhere, somehow. I remember standing in my kitchen, either the day she died or the day after, and literally wailing aloud: "Dear God! Please! Let me know she's okay! I need to see a vision. I need to hear a voice." I literally felt desperate to obtain proof that she was still around somehow—I loved her that much. So I poured out my grieving heart to the Lord in that kitchen.

That night I went to sleep, and in the middle of the night, I was awakened by the sound of wind chimes. But I was only awakened partway—to that state between awake and sleep. It seemed like time was suspended for the next few moments. Anyway, these wind chimes were like a signal to me to pay attention. We do not own any wind chimes; there were no wind chimes hanging inside or outside the house. I heard the loud sound in my head and inside the room that I was in. Then I heard Nana's voice, loud and clear. I also saw a dim image or vision of her face in front of my face. It was not a clear vision, just an added indication to me that it was her speaking. Her voice filled the whole room. And there was no mistaking it; nobody could reproduce this voice. It was her actual voice, and she sounded more alive, vital, and healthy than ever! She simply said (and not too quickly): "Hello, Lisa." I remember the exact tone and inflection when she said that. It was almost like: "You poor dear. Here I am. If you really need to hear me, here I am." Her words liter-

ally filled the whole room and me. I could not deny that I heard her voice, that she was indeed alive. Following her "hello" statement, she said one more thing that I can't quite remember. It was a statement of reassurance; either "I'm fine," "I'm okay," or "I love you." But the "Hello, Lisa" was all I needed. From that point on, I don't think I ever shed one more tear of grief for Nana. Why should I? I knew she was alive, and that I will see her again someday.

Lisa's experience reordered her inner life, strengthening her faith and beliefs in an afterlife and the world of the spirit. Her Extraordinary Encounter forced her to refocus on the state of her soul, and helped her turn inward to find the strength to grow through and transcend her grief. "When I ponder how the experience has affected my life," she said, "I discover that I have a keener sense that our time on earth is limited and that we need to use our time wisely. I don't want to waste it. I have also learned that when a person dies, his or her love for people still on earth continues. It never ends. And the relationships continue in loving form." These new continuing relationships, the re-connections with deceased loved ones, have a major impact on the strength and direction of mourners' inner lives and ultimate happiness.

The Importance of the Inner Life

Many years ago I was reading an article in a prestigious journal and came across a statement made by a Canadian psychiatrist that has stuck with me through the years. He said, "There is only one mental illness, a wrong perception of the Self." It caught me off guard at first, but then, as I continued to think about it, it revealed to me a profound truth: So many of us have inaccurate pictures of ourselves. The way we think about ourselves influences everything we do, especially the way we deal with loss and change. I have seen so many people in the throes of dealing with the loss of a cherished love one through death, separation, or divorce, who believed they were worthless and incapable of happiness. The result was almost always inaction, isolation, and eventual illness of one type or another—all due to a decline in the quality of the inner life initiated by a wrong perception of the self. They convinced themselves that all was lost, that they could never be happy again.

I'm here to tell you just the opposite. We all have the ability—and the right—to regain peace and happiness after loss. Resiliency is part of our nature; we can and eventually will embrace life again. Remember what we talked about in

Chapters 3 and 5? First: *What you focus on expands.* What you feel is a result of what you think, not the other way around. Second: *Action heals.* Recovering from grief starts with taking first steps toward the creation of new routines, relationships, activities, etc. Together those two concepts make up what I call your "inner work": realigning your positive thoughts and preparing yourself to act on them. Your thoughts are the most powerful forces at your disposal in your quest to find meaning in life and cope with feelings of emptiness. It's your thoughts, and the actions that follow, that create your reality. And nothing can destroy your thoughts, your inner work, except for you. That's why you need to pay close attention to your prize possession, your inner dialogue. If you are unhappy, change the message your mind is sending your body and alter what you do. Happiness will find you.

That's right—happiness will find you. Don't try to look for it, because you won't find it. At least, not until you complete your inner work. Happiness is a by-product of what we do in the present moment. Build and rebuild your inner life. Change the beliefs that give birth to negative behavior ("I'll never recover from this loss," or "I'll never be happy again without my loved one") and you will feel better. Eventually, joy will emerge from your heart.

Remember—happiness isn't something we can get from possessions, or even the people around us. Sometimes we forget that we are *created as free and happy beings*, and instead get sold on the idea that we need all sorts of products and inventions to keep us satisfied. The opposite is true. You can do more and be more with less. Once you realize that, you can define yourself by simplicity and your inherent abilities to decide what is truly essential to live well. When you release yourself from your attachments to people and possessions, you automatically reshape your reality for the better.

I want to talk about the idea of attachment a little bit more. It's very important for mourners to learn that love and attachment are not the same thing. Love is being fully committed to the welfare of the beloved; attachment is binding, constricting, being concerned with how objects or the beloved meet your needs. Take a moment to look at your own life. Are you dependent on things or people for your happiness? Have you fallen into the trap of letting other people determine your thoughts, actions, your sense of well-being? That kind of attachment is the inevitable prelude to unnecessary pain and suffering.

Attachment sets conditions for joy and happiness, conditions that are bound to be broken. Change must and will happen. Conditions and circumstances will always be in flux. People will not always be what you want them to be. Some will come through for you, but others will let you down. That's why attachment can never bring you true happiness. Let go of the conditioned belief that things or people can make you happy. When you do, you'll see that, because true happiness comes from within, you *can* love the people, places, and things in your life even though you fully understand you will not have all you possess forever.

I'm constantly reminded of the wisdom of Epictetus, the first-century stoic, who said in the *Enchiridion* that "Men are disturbed not by things, but by the views they take of them." What a powerful thought. We *do* have the ability to choose to be happy long before events occur that are conditioned signals to be unhappy. The key is to become a master of what I call "reframing," that is, changing the way you percieve or give meaning to an event. In short, altering the course of how you were *conditioned* to experience it. I know it is a difficult concept to understand at first, but coping well with the loss of a loved one is more a matter of making good choices and embracing alternative meanings than anything else. Everything that happens to you as you adjust to your loss, every problem and every mood you experience, will be the result of the choices you make. You can choose to nurture the ache in your heart or limit its effects. You can choose to resist change—try to control the uncontrollable—and be sad forever in your self-imposed prison, or learn to open your heart and find joy again. You can choose to start a new life with inner peace as your primary goal, or remain trapped in the time machine of the past. You can make those choices; you can do your inner work; you can strengthen your inner life, just like Lisa did, after she made the choice to release her grief about her husband's grandmother's death.

How to Strengthen Your Inner Life

1. **Feed on inspirational themes.** We need good food for the mind as well as the body, especially inspirational food that can counter the endless negative and depressing themes we find on the airwaves. You might purchase a small book of daily inspirational sayings, poetry, or prayers (available in any bookstore). Put the book in a place where you will see it and use it daily. Make every effort to expand and improve your perspective, to center yourself, and you'll find yourself developing an important inner skill— nurturing a hopeful heart. Hope and faith have always

been major factors in physical health and happiness because of the sense of meaning they generate. And constantly renewing your faith is an absolute must when you're dealing with loss and change. Your daily inspirations will help take your inner critic out of the picture and feed your soul.

As a final note, consider pasting this quote by the great novelist and Nobel Prize–winner Pearl Buck on the cover of your book of daily inspirations: "Inside myself is a place where I live all alone, and that's where I renew my springs that never dry up."

2. Recognize your thought traps. It's a good idea not to take *anything* personally, with one exception—what you say to yourself. Unhappy people spend lots of time thinking and talking to themselves about their losses long after they occur. Conversely, happy people spend more time thinking about the things that keep them up and inspired. Don't underestimate the importance of the conversations you have with yourself and the effect they have on how you see the outer world. These inner conversations bring the negative or positive in your life to full force. Especially when you're dealing with loss, repeating negative thoughts in your mind and heart—thoughts like "I'm not good at dealing with change," "I can't do it without him/her," or

"What did I do to have this happen to me?"—destroys your ability to act confidently and decisively, to do the inner work I talked about earlier. Oppose your inner critic with your inner cheerleader; change the way you talk to yourself. Get rid of words like *can't* or *never*. Replace them with *will* and *am*.

The solution to breaking the pattern of negative thinking is to point out to yourself *why a particular thought is wrong*. When you hear yourself saying, "I can't let go of my hurt," challenge it with "I have not yet been able to let go of my hurt (following whatever loss), but I vow to begin releasing it right now." Use words like "I vow" or "I commit" to reflect the strong commitment to recovery you're willing to make.

Another very specific thing you can do is establish a set "worry time," a twenty- to thirty-minute period each day where you fully place your attention on situations you are concerned about. Write down ideas for concrete steps you can do to fix the problematic situations. If you can't think of any, write down affirmations that remind you that you will be able to overcome the situation. There is research that says chronic worriers who spend a set amount of time daily actively focusing on their worries actually experience less worry over time. When they start to worry at other times, they can remind themselves that they can think about those issues at the next "worry time," and quickly turn their attention elsewhere. That simple action helps them reduce their overall level of anxiety.

3. Develop your contemplative skills. Push your "Off button" every day by developing a daily stress-reduction routine to cut into the constant barrage of painful thoughts associated with your loss. Take a walk. Do some yoga. Turn off the telephone and close the door to your room. It doesn't have to be for long—twenty or thirty minutes will do. The point is, although we can't avoid stress altogether, we can use our contemplative skills to take much-needed time-outs from reality, periods of important psychological and physical recharging.

A big part of developing your contemplative skills is enabling your imagination, the creative genius of the mind, and the basis for all great accomplishment. I believe the imagination is the cornerstone for building whatever you want in life. If you take control of your imagination, use it to create images of what you want out of life and encourage your ability to see the glass half full, you can write your own scripts. Here's an exercise I give many of the people who come to see me: Imagine being in your own personal paradise. If you need to, look at a picture in a magazine or an old photo to stimulate the imagery. Carefully examine every part of the landscape in your mind. See all the colors. Smell the aromas around you. Let yourself be flooded with the feelings and emotions being in that place stirs in you. If stressful thoughts reappear, don't become alarmed. Simply let them go—dispatch them to "worry time," and continue on with your imaginative journey. Stay in your mental paradise for ten minutes before you bring yourself back to reality. See how much more relaxed you feel?

You may be more disposed to meditation as a contemplative skill, as suggested in Chapter 4. Or perhaps you're more affected by yet another contemplative ability— breathing work. If you can become skilled at observing and changing your breathing patterns, you'll possess a powerful weapon for dealing with tension, anger, and anxiety. To begin breathing work, sit in a restful position, your back comfortably straight, and focus on slowing each inhalation and exhalation. Find a word or phrase that is most meaningful to you. For instance, you might try the phrase *Slow down* or *Release*. When I awake in the middle of the night and can't get back to sleep, the single word I repeat is *Sleep* each time I exhale. When I feel my heart beating too fast, I slowly say, "Heart slow down." Find your breathing rate and slow it down as much as you can; each time you exhale, repeat your word or phrase.

4. Use nature as a form of therapy. The beauty of nature holds great truths and is full of transcendent meaning: symbols of rebirth, change, inexhaustible mystery, and eternal renewal. Isolating yourself from nature, like isolating yourself from human interaction, is damaging to your emotional life. So when you're feeling low and distressed, look for a moment of awakening in the sounds and colors of nature. Find a quiet spot and stay there for at least an hour. Study the details of the environment and feel the peace of beauty flow into you, soothing and healing, giving you respite from your grief.

Many people I've met believe that beauty is "your Higher Power remembering you." So look for the hidden face of your Higher Power in the stunning blue sky; the brilliant white cloud formations or the giant thunderheads; in stilt-legged blue herons flying gracefully over a marsh; in the warmth of the jeweled sun; in the smell of freshly mowed grass, or the flourishing flowers. Rise early (you're probably awake anyway, if you're in the throes of mourning) and watch a sunrise. If you're near the seashore, savor the beauty of the scattered seashells, the vast ocean, or a boat in full sail.

But wait! Don't discount the power of healing in the beauty of "ordinary" nature. If you've been forced to move due to your loss, make it a high priority to move into a new house or apartment with a view of trees and grass. Spend as much time as possible outside in your neighborhood, or if nothing else, in a room with a window. Whether at home, in the hospital, or at a vacation house, a room with a view will bring your attention to the beauty and peacefulness of the universe around you.

5. **Nurture your intuition.** Have you ever had one of those flashes, where it was suddenly clear what you wanted or had to do? That's intuition—the instant grasping of reality, a lightbulb going on as you find a solution to a problem, the gut feeling that you should take a specific course of action. Sudden insights, hunches, and feelings are all ways in which the unconscious (some believe a Higher Power) brings useful information to our conscious awareness. Most of us already know that gut feelings play a crucial role in every major decision we make, from relationships to finances. But many of us may not understand that we have a responsibility to develop our relationship with intuition—to learn how to better use gut feelings, sudden insights, synchronicities, dreams, visions, to make better choices. Coping well with loss always involves *rising above your previous level of awareness*, and intuition, which is part of your spiritual intelligence, will help you do just that.

So, how can you develop intuitive self-reliance? First, you have to listen more closely to your inner voice and the feelings that often accompany it. Then, practice by learning to recognize patterns and cues that emerge when you make decisions. Force yourself to integrate what your insides are saying with what your logical mind is dictating. When you're presented with a specific problem, ask yourself what your gut is telling you—you can trust that it will be the truth. Learn to be more sensitive to the physical and mental signals that accompany an intuitive presence. Pay attention to the mental pictures or ideas that pop into your head when you're confronting a problem, the sensations in your body when someone is talking to you. Give yourself the freedom to make a decision based on a "eureka moment."

Here's one intuitive exercise I give many of the people who come to me for counseling: The next time you have a weighty decision to make, find a quiet place away from distractions. Review the rational reasons for making the decision, whatever they may be. Then ask yourself, "What should I do?" to bring out your intuitive feelings. Let the feelings, urges, and hunches of what is right or wrong come out in full force. Examine your rational options in light of your intuitive thoughts, and if possible, try to blend the two together. You may decide to go with your intuition alone, or your rational mind or a combination of both. The important thing is that you always remember how powerful a tool intuition can be. When your intuitive feelings surface, don't overanalyze them. Information will come to you suddenly. In the middle of your grief work, when you least expect them, you'll receive new insights. Honor them.

6. Keep a journal. Whether you fill it with personal thoughts and feelings, memories, or prayers, a journal can be an effective means of enhancing your inner dialogue and your overall spirituality. (For an example, see the best-selling novelist Andrew Greeley's *Windows: A Prayer Journal.*) In your journal, you can let the universe know what's bothering you, ask for advice, complain a little bit, recap the day, give thanks, ask for the wisdom and insight to make upcoming decisions, even record the answers you receive to your wishes or prayers of petition. Make a list of the positive things in your life; ask for the courage and grace to eliminate the negatives. Record the insights, reflections, and ideas that pop into your mind. You might even write letters to whoever is a current source of deep emotion in your life, whether alive or dead.

Your journal is a place where you can explore your deepest feelings. You can confess your faults and express the unthinkable. If you feel unloved, say so. Nothing is off limits—just tell it like it is. Remember, if you write freely, you will develop a stronger relationship with your Higher Power and your inner self. In that way, you should think of journaling as one of your daily spiritual practices. It doesn't matter how you do it—you can write in a notebook or on a computer, if you prefer. In any case, don't worry about your writing ability; just write. And as you're journaling, be sure to date each entry so that every month or two, you can go back and see what you wrote, and notice how you have progressed and how the patterns of your life have changed. Soon you'll be able to see just how far you've come. I promise, writing will lead to self-discovery. You will learn so much about yourself to use in the pursuit of your mission and purpose in life.

7. Strive to imprint and maintain powerful memories. Though commonly taken for granted, memory plays an essential role in both learning and healing because of the way it factors into how we perceive the events around us. What you choose to recall drastically effects how you live your life in the present: how you remain in contact with deceased loved ones, how you learn from the past, and perhaps most importantly, how you use good memories to bring you lasting joy and empower your life. Willa Cather,

considered one of the great American writers of the twen-
tieth century, contends that "Some memories are realities,
and are better than anything that can ever happen to one
again." Her point is that good memories can be powerful
sources of comfort and joy. They can also be very real
points of connection to deceased loved ones, because the
significance, insight, and identity of the deceased grow
through remembrance. In that way, remembrance practices can become an integral part of family life from generation to generation.

Take an inventory of your inner self and recall the
happy memories of love and belonging from your past, especially those involving your deceased loved one, and
think of the wisdom and encouragement you gained.
When you are ready, revisit special places, reread old letters, look over collected mementos, pictures, or scrap-
books, read something your loved one use to read, play
some of your old favorite songs, think of a movie you
watched together, or seek out friends and relatives who are
willing to talk about memories of your loved one. Write
down your most pleasing recollections, and then decide
on a word or phrase that will bring those specific events
into your consciousness whenever you need them. Start
the habit of invoking those specific memories when you're
feeling low. Remember, reminiscing is healthy—not a way

of living in the past, but rather a way of appreciating all you have experienced and accomplished.

How do you take short-term memories and make them a permanent part of your long-term memory? The answer is repetition (which actually causes structural changes in the brain). We have a tendency to remember what we keep thinking about. Rely on memory aids: a picture, a glass, a golf ball, a special book. Almost anything can be a cue for remembering a person, a trip you enjoyed, a special gift you received, something that was left to you, or something you learned that will forever be cherished. Of course, EEs can be powerful memory-makers, as well as major factors in building an adequate defense against the stress and the anxiety that accompanies the grief process. Recording your EEs can help you reposition your perspective and keep you grounded; recreating EEs in your mind after the fact can be an effective way to deal with loneliness and sadness. If you have had an EE, consider making a memory card to record your experience in detail, and use it as a reminder that you have been given a gift. That alone is a memory to cherish.

By the same token, you must be aware that constantly dwelling on sad memories will have the same effect— you're going to retain them if you constantly repeat them in your mind. In fact, a tremendous amount of unnecessary suffering comes from recalling memories that cause ill feelings and generate anxiety. These bad memories stick with us because we tend to experience negative emotions more strongly than positive ones, and they're just as strong months or even years later. Let tears come, if you feel like it. Then stop; readjust your mind; and take delight in a loving memory of the person.

Recall what I said in Chapter 3: Your past doesn't automatically determine your future—unless you allow it to. Even if you had a conflicting or abusive relationship with the deceased, it's possible to find a few good memories to balance your recollections. Take time to identify the painful memories you've inherited from people who influenced you early in life or that are associated with the loss you're mourning. Recognize that memories connected with passionate emotions take longer to purge and release. Then try the following: Each time you are drawn to a stressful memory, see yourself there with one added difference. See yourself back in the moment, but instead of being alone, you are standing next to your best friend, Jesus, Buddha—whoever gives you the most strength. Visualize that Being supporting you, talking to you, easing your painful feelings, suggesting forgiveness if necessary; allow the experience to release its power over you. If there is a specific person involved with the painful memory, include him or her in your visualization as you forgive. Start repeating this exercise today, and see how it gradually reduces the pain and anxiety of the unpleasant memories you experience.

TAKING ONE STEP AT A TIME

By now I hope you understand how critical it is to commit yourself to finding joy by strengthening your inner life. But I hope you also realize how much work there is to do. You can't expect to take everything I talked about in this chapter on at once and have immediate success. Break it down into specifics. Take one or two of the seven steps above and start the process.

For example, say you want to work on recognizing and overcoming the thought trigger that makes you feel lonely (Step 2). First, identify the trigger. Is it seeing your best friend out with her husband? Walking by your loved one's photo on the mantel? Whatever it is, decide what you're going to do when the cascade of lonely feelings invade your thinking. What actions will you take? Prepare a schedule of activities for each day, including such mundane things as cleaning, window shopping, reading, watching TV, visiting friends, gardening, walking, etc. Be ready to act quickly and decisively when you feel your emotional trigger start to loom.

The most important thing is that you don't expect perfection. Everyone experiences failure at one point or another. Remember the metaphor I used in Chapter 5? Think of coping with grief as an endurance race—you have to hang in there through the ups and downs until you get your big second wind. So even if you have a bad day—one of those days where you really feel you're "losing it"—don't dwell on it. Grief is a very stressful emotion, and sometimes your body just has to take a break. Those days are when your automatic shut-off valve kicks in and says, "Step back, slow down, take a rest." You can't keep running on empty forever. That's the time to sit back and engage in some of the contemplative skills I talked about in Step 3. You'll come back stronger and more determined the next day.

There's just one more important thing you have to do: If you want the new behavior you have been working on to stick and your inner life to grow, each day you succeed, give yourself rewards for your successes. There are many spiritual victories on the journey of grief you can celebrate: getting through the "year of the firsts" without your loved one, taking on new responsibilities, making new friends, joining a support group. Recognize your progress and reward yourself accordingly.

The joy you feel from your inner life will grow even more when you take to heart the sixth wisdom lesson from the realm of the extraordinary: giving generously, the topic of the next chapter.

*A person cannot directly choose his circumstances,
but he can choose his thoughts, and so indirectly, yet
surely, shape his circumstances.*

—JAMES ALLEN 1864–1920, AUTHOR OF *AS A MAN THINKETH*

CHAPTER SEVEN

CHOOSE TO SERVE

I slept and dreamt that life was joy. I awoke and saw that life was service. I acted and behold, service was joy.

—RABINDRANATH TAGORE

We make a living by what we get, we make a life by what we give.

—WINSTON CHURCHILL

The underlying theme of Chapter 6 was that a strong inner life ultimately helps us find joy and cope well with loss and change. The underlying theme of *this* chapter is that the simple act of giving is a boon to the coping process because of the positive inner feelings it generates and the connections with others it produces. Together, a strong inner life, permeated with a commitment of service to others, will transform your journey of adjusting to loss.

As the ancient Chinese proverb goes, if you want to find joy . . .

. . . for an hour, take a nap.

. . . for a day, go fishing.

. . . for a month, get married.

. . . for a year, get an inheritance.

. . . for a lifetime, help someone.

But before we talk about how you, as mourners, can serve others, I want to make one point clear. All Extraordinary Encounters are gifts—gifts from our deceased loved ones or a Higher Power. There are different ways to serve, different ways to help people. For those who have died, the greatest gifts are gestures of solace to those grieving their loss. Read these next two stories; see how far these departed loved ones went to give the gift of comfort to the people they left behind.

Will anyone forget where they were that morning of September 11, 2001? I suspect not. Our two sons, Andrew and Michael, both worked in New York in the brokerage business. They had worked together at Cantor-Fitzgerald on the 104th floor of the World Trade Center until nine months before that fateful day (when Michael had accepted an offer from Prudential and started working in another building in lower Manhattan). I cannot tell you how precious Andy was. He was our first male, born after four girls and on his father's birthday. From the earliest times of his life he had been a joy, extremely outgoing and loving, and as he grew his sense of humor developed, making him the kind of person others were drawn to. His younger brother Michael, born two and a half years later, idolized him. Despite the age difference, they were together constantly. Mike even followed his brother to the University of Maryland.

That morning a distraught Mike called to say that a plane had just struck Tower One of the WTC. He was leaving his building to go over there to check on his brother Andy. He wanted to know if Andy's wife, Christine, had called. I said no but I would immediately go to their house in Middletown, which was about thirty-five minutes away. My husband, Bob, and I turned on the television and at that point the major networks were all carrying the picture—the horrific picture that will forever burn in our memories.

I arrived at the house. Chris had heard the news of the attack, but did not want to watch the TV. She had received a telephone call from Andy with the short message, "Our building has been hit by a plane. I'm alive and I love you," but that was the last we had heard from him. I fed Robert Andrew (named after his Dad) who had been born three weeks previously. I was glued to the television—hypnotically so—somehow hoping for a miracle repeating my prayer to the Lord, "Thy will be done."

Just about noon I went to the kitchen to put a bottle on for Robert and suddenly a vision flashed into my mind—a beautiful blue background and a stick figure of glowing light, with its arms raised, ascending upward. I knew then that Andy had passed to the next life. I did all I could do not to break down and sob, as Chris was still so hopeful that he would be rescued. We needed to do that much for her—not to give up that hope until she was ready.

By the seventh day Chris had still not given up hope that Andy would be found. Nevertheless, we arranged for a Mass to be said for just the family at our home. This allowed us to grieve outwardly and together. I alternated with Chris's mother, spending day and night with my daughter-in-law. I believe the outpouring of love and caring from so many people helped her keep from breaking down that first week. The girls (ages three and five) had been told that Daddy couldn't get home yet because there had been an accident in the building where he worked. They were so upset, crying for Daddy to come home. He had been such a "hands-on" father, reading and roughhousing with them. Shortly after the

Mass, Chris knew she had to admit he had died. She drove to a nearby beach to walk. When she parked the car, it was surrounded by a swarm of fluttering butterflies. She came back somewhat comforted that this may have been a sign from Andy that he lived on in a new dimension. (Since that time, she and the girls have seen butterflies at enough odd times that they take it as a sign that Daddy is still watching over them.)

I started taking Robert to our house on the weekends, feeling Chris needed all the rest she could get. It must have been a month after Andy's death that I had the baby in his carrier on our kitchen table. My husband, Bob, called me over to the window to look out at a hawk seated on a low branch in our backyard. We had seen no other hawks with the exception of two summers before, when a baby hawk was unable to fly and we had called the animal control officer to provide assistance for it. When I saw this bird on a branch at most fifteen to twenty feet high, I immediately thought that it somehow was another sign that Andy was watching over his son.

Now, my heritage is all Irish, and I recognize a tendency in myself to be "fey" (having visionary power; clairvoyant). I am a believer in the possibility of what some would consider totally unprovable happenings. Knowing this about myself, I said a prayer that if it was just my imagination, the bird would fly away when I attempted to go to the tree. If not, I would consider it a true sign. I opened the door to the deck and was able to walk right under the branch. The hawk followed my movements with his eyes but never moved from his perch. I cannot tell you what joy and thanksgiving poured through me at that time. The hawk stayed in the tree for another hour.

More reinforcement came eight months later with an incident at the library. That day I headed to the shelves to see if there was anything new by a favorite author. I found one book. Also in this section were Nelson De Mille's books, and I found one of his I hadn't read, as well. As I glanced through both books, trying to decide which one I wanted to read first, a bookmark fell out of one of them. I picked it up and looked at it—on the front was a little blue bird surrounded by red hearts and the words "Love can reach above the heavens." I knew then, and will always believe, that this message was an incredible gift from Andy. With the thousands of books in our library I could have picked, it was no coincidence I chose that one at random. Tears streamed down my face and joy filled my heart at God's goodness.

Two and a half years have passed, but not a day goes by without thoughts and memories of Andy flooding my *mind. Life has had its ups and downs, but that loss was the most devastating experience we have ever had. Yet many blessings have been ours as well. We have our grandchildren, our faith has deepened, and we have reached out to others suffering the loss of a loved one. I do believe that what so many call coincidences are anything but. When we are dealing with incredible loss, if we are truly open to possibilities, we will be comforted. We will never truly know the infinite wonder and love our Creator has for each one of us, but we do catch glimpses of His love and caring if we open our eyes and our hearts. I have no fear of death. Bob and I are so grateful for this wonderful son who had lived so fully in his thirty-five years and became what we believe God intended him to be—a wonderful son, brother, husband, and friend to so many. And even in death he has given freely after leaving us.*

—Pat Spencer, Piscataway, New Jersey

And here's the second story . . .

My husband, Tom, and I were married in May 1999, and moved to a house in the country. He had always wanted to live in the country and was very happy there. Unfortunately, nine months after our marriage, my hus-

band was diagnosed with advanced cancer. He passed away in November 2001. My husband's biggest fear when he was dying was what was going to happen to me. He was very worried about how I would manage without him, as he always felt it was his job to take care of me and watch over me. When I realized there was no hope for him to survive, I tried to reassure him that there was a life after death and that he would still be able to watch over me from the other side. I told him that I would be okay just as long as I knew he was there, and I asked him if there was any way he could give me some kind of sign after he died—then I would be all right.

Two days after Tom passed away, I received my first sign. I had gone to bed and woke up in the middle of the night and looked at the clock. It was 3:30 A.M. I was lying in bed trying to get back to sleep when I suddenly felt the blankets pulling me as though trying to face me in the other direction. I was a little frightened but said to myself, "Okay, let's just go with this and see what happens." On turning, I saw Tom. He was sitting cross-legged in the air in the corner of the bedroom over the dog's crate. He was leaning over and it looked like he was trying to light a cigarette. The funny part was that Tom had not smoked in over twenty years, though he had often told me that he never had lost his craving for cigarettes, and if he didn't know it was bad for him, it would be easy to start again. I actually hadn't known him when he smoked, so it was odd that I would have pictured him doing it. And sure enough, for the rest of the experience, I no longer saw him with the cigarette or observed him smoking. I think it was just something to catch my attention, to show me I was actually seeing him.

Tom looked like he did before he got sick. He had his weight back and his hair, and he looked good. He was wearing jeans and a gray sweater, which was one of his favorites. I looked at him and said in my mind, not out loud, "Tom, is it really you?" With that, one side of him changed—suddenly he was wearing a ripped T-shirt, and he started shaking his shoulder and doing a sexy little maneuver. This was typical of him, as he always liked to fool around. I laughed and said, again in my head, "Okay, it's you." Then he pointed at me, put two fingers out, and pointed up. I got a little upset because I thought he was telling me I was going to die soon, too. He just smiled and did the same motion again, and I realized what he was telling me was that someday I would be where he is and that he would be there waiting. Then he just disappeared. I was wide awake and afraid to move. My heart was pounding like crazy. My sister was *sleeping in the next room, so I finally got up and went into her room and told her what had happened.*

The night of the funeral, which was two nights later, I had another experience. I again woke up at around the same time. All of a sudden I felt myself being moved in the bed. It felt like I was rotated completely around, so that my head was facing the bottom of the bed, and then back around again. Then I felt a strong pressure on my hand, like Tom was holding my hand. This lasted a few seconds. I felt no fear, just felt very relaxed and peaceful, and I knew it was him saying his good-byes. These experiences really helped me get through the funeral, as I knew my husband was still around and watching over me.

Since then I have had other things happen which cannot be explained and I know are signs that he is still taking care of me. I will give you one example. I recently took a temporary job assignment near Boston. When I was moving into my new apartment, I lost the key to the lobby entrance. Most likely, I accidentally left it in the door—something I often did. When he was alive, Tom was always reminding me about it, telling me I wasn't streetwise. Luckily, my sister had gone up to Boston with me to help me move, so she also had a set of keys.

The next day I planned to go back home to bring

more things up; my sister was going to stay in the apartment. We were discussing what to do about the lost key, as I would have no way to get back in without a key and she needed the other one to go in and out of the apartment. As I was standing there discussing the situation with her, I felt something in my shoe. I was wearing laced sneakers and had been up for several hours; I had even gone out and walked the dog. But when I looked inside my sneaker, directly under the middle of my foot, I found the missing key. I had not been wearing those sneakers the day before, when I lost the key—in fact, they were in a corner in my bedroom, nowhere near where I could have dropped the key. And I certainly would have felt the key sooner if it had been in my shoe when I put it on. I know it was my husband reminding me to be more careful, as he often did when he was alive. He purposely caused the key to appear in a place where it was impossible to be so that I could be sure it was a sign from him.

I know my husband is still around and still watching over me. That knowledge has given me great comfort and helped me through these difficult times. Death is not the end. Working as a nurse, I often encounter people who are very sick and dying, and I try to reassure them that life does continue. I don't push my beliefs on

anyone, but if they are open and receptive, knowing that
these things can and do happen can be comforting when
they are facing the possibility of death.
　　　　　　　　—*Joan Farrell, Lakeville, Connecticut*

Isn't it easy to see how Extraordinary Encounters are acts of service, acts of generosity in the deepest sense of the word? They are gifts from our departed loved ones, given freely and entirely out of love. In the beauty and timeliness of these encounters, we can see how profoundly the givers had the recipients at heart.

But now, let's look at how else these stories express a message of service. For the grief-stricken widow, the EE was not only a dramatic example of loving reassurance from her husband, Tom, about life after death, but also a reminder that she too could give reassurance to others through her vocation as a nurse. The grieving mother was not only given the gift of acceptance, but she was also released from the burden of her anger at the terrorists, a fact she later confided in me. She was able to find solace in the blessings she received, even in the midst of such a tragic ordeal.

That's the lesson that we, as mourners, have to learn— there is healing power in giving. And in giving and healing, we can find not only solace and the comfort of having helped another person in need, but also, eventually, true happiness from within.

Finding Healing in Giving

It is one of those beautiful compensations of life that no one can sincerely try to help another without helping himself.

—RALPH WALDO EMERSON

It's easy to overlook the importance of giving (something embraced by almost all of the major spiritual traditions in the world), especially when you're in the grips of mourning. But I believe that once you start, you'll realize just how much you have to give—which will in turn allow your inner strength to come to light. Aches and pains have a way of disappearing; peace and comfort have a way of coming back.

Allan Luks, author of *The Healing Power of Doing Good,* conducted a study of more than three thousand volunteers from big cities to rural areas and found that 95 percent of those who had regular contact with people they helped experienced an inner feeling that he dubbed the "helper's high." (Recent studies have shown this high to be the result of an increase in the "feel good" neurotransmitter serotonin. Kindness was shown to raise serotonin levels and strengthen the immune system in both the giver, and incredibly, the receiver, too.) Over the long run the experience of helping translated into greater self-worth, stress reduction, and similar long-term health benefits to those resulting from meditation or simple relaxation. Luks found the increased social ties developed through service enhanced the server's emotional and physical health. Further research has shown that those who regularly help others reap the benefits of reduced depression, less fatigue, fewer headaches and backaches, an increased sense of control, and more general satisfaction with life.

Those findings suggest, as I believe, that our self-worth is not merely a product of people telling us that we are important or wonderful. Rather, it is the result of the things we do, the way we sincerely contribute to the world. Human suffering is everywhere, but in doing your part to reduce it, you can simultaneously reduce your pain. Your altruistic behavior will not only help others, but also light the fire of inner peace that will lead to a healthier you. You'll find giving to be an antidote for the sense of powerlessness that accompanies your losses. And it is through giving that you will find yourself again, manage your sorrow, free yourself from isolation, and bring intimacy back into your life.

Now, I don't expect all this giving to happen immediately after the loss of a loved one. You're going to need some time to grieve on your own, to do some of the inner work we talked about in earlier chapters. But when the time is right, when your wounds are not as raw, you will be able to reach out and give back. You will confront—either consciously or unconsciously—the pivotal question all mourners eventually face: "Will I be loss oriented or restoration oriented?" Will you make sorrow your way of life, or will you choose a path to peace? Will you be a prisoner of your own thoughts, or will you find freedom through service? Are you content with only being wounded, or will you instead become a wounded healer? Remember, you don't have to *feel* like giving to be an effective giver. Knowing you're doing the right thing, even when you have to push yourself to do it, is of greater value to your healing. For that's commitment at its highest level. Deep within, when you review your day, you will feel a real sense of accomplishment and gain.

What to Give

So, how do you go about making this transition in your grief process? How do you figure out when, what, and how you're ready to serve? The first step is to start each day thinking *What can I give?* Open your eyes as well as your heart. When you see a need, don't hesitate—just fill it. Ask yourself what gifts you have to give to the world, to your community, to your family. Everyone has something to give. Simple things—like a welcoming smile, recognizing a job well done, making a telephone call, writing a thank-you note, or dropping a postcard in the mail—can make a huge difference in someone's day. Think of someone you know in a nursing home or assisted living facility, or a child without parents who would appreciate your time.

Of course, there's always someone who, like you, is mourning the death of a loved one or another major loss, possibly in silence. But you can change that with something as simple as a telephone call. As one widow in a support group confided, "I long to hear from somebody." A few minutes of conversation really can mean the world to someone who is alone. Don't underestimate how effective it can be! I've made it a cornerstone of my grief therapy. In every support group I conduct, at the end of each session, we draw names of group members. Sometime during the following week, each person calls the person whose name he or she drew.

You will always be able to find opportunities to interact with others, if you only establish the habit of looking for them. Stay alert for chances to speak first and give one of what I like to call the Big Four: a wave, a "Hi" (using the person's first name whenever possible), a hug, or a handshake. Make a list of other "things" you can give with little effort, whether physical or emotional, and keep it in a visible place in your home. Here are some easy examples.

- Appreciation
- Attention
- Admiration
- Blood
- Compliments
- Crafts
- Encouragement
- Flowers
- Food
- Gifts
- Ideas
- I love yous
- Joy
- Peace
- Prayers
- Recognition
- Respect
- Time
- Toys
- Thank-yous

The next step is to decide what specific behaviors you will use to give those things away. For example, what will you say to show your admiration for someone? How will you give that precious appreciation and attention we all crave? Approval is absolutely essential for our emotional health—

everyone needs it from the right person and at the right time. *You* are the right person.

DEVELOPING AN ATTITUDE OF SERVICE

Beyond the general ideas I listed above, here are six suggestions for developing an overall attitude of service that will lead to helping others, and at the same time help you deal with all the changes you face without your loved one. Always remember, if you live generously, you *will* be able to integrate your loss into your life.

1. Give something away each day. This isn't as hard as it first may seem. Review the list in the previous section. You always have something to give—it's simply a matter of being generous with what you have. You can give time (visit someone at the nursing home or hospital), appreciation (give someone a pleasant smile), food (most everyone loves baked goods!), experience (share a life story with a friend), unused books or clothing, companionship, trust, a thank-you—the list is endless. Divide your list into the things you can start doing right away, and those that will take more time and preparation to carry out. Start planning now. And always keep an idea fresh in your mind so that you have it at the top of your "to do" list each day.

"Make it your guiding principle," said Confucius, "to do your best for others." You might not always see the end result of your generosity, but you can be assured it will change you and be a step forward on your path out of darkness.

2. Teach someone a skill that you possess. *Everyone has something to teach.* There's a story about Sherwood Anderson, the author of the widely praised novel *Winesburg, Ohio*, who was always willing to help young writers. A young aspiring writer took an apartment near him in Chicago, and started bringing him samples of his writing for critiques. Anderson gave generously of his time, though he was brutal with his assessment. But because of his willingness to teach his skill, a new writer came on the scene. His name: Ernest Hemingway.

If you are a good cook, athlete, mason, chess player, seamstress, storyteller, whatever, pass your skills and insight on to another. Give those around you the benefits of what life has taught you, and you'll empower them to perpetuate that knowledge through another generation. And don't forget how important sharing you EEs can be, especially to the young, on whom such stories can have a powerful impact. Throughout civilization, values and wisdom have been passed on through stories. Don't be afraid to take your place in that tradition.

3. Be proactive. Look for opportunities to give, and when you find one, act decisively, without fanfare. Mother Teresa once said, "Do not wait for leaders. Do it alone, person to person." To put this wisdom into practice, simply start off deciding that every day you will assess one situation and decide what you can do in a small way to make it better. Whether it's just by being polite, giving moral support, recognizing someone else's good deed, or giving a helping hand to someone who is handicapped or has their arms full, the key is to develop the ability to *recognize opportunity* and discreetly take advantage of it. Think about how you might improve the lives of your neighbors. And don't overlook the elderly. Recent research shows the staggering need older Americans have for help with simple activities like cooking, shopping, and housework.

4. Sign up for volunteer activities. Soup kitchens, shelters for abused women, hospitals. Relief centers for natural disasters like hurricanes, floods, and fires. Community programs offered by colleges and churches, as well as counties and cities. Youth sports teams, recreation centers, yoga centers. The opportunities for volunteer work abound. And the great thing about volunteering is, even as you're giving back in a significant way to your community, you can do wonders for your social life! You'll be surprised how many friends you can make who have similar interests. Try it—I promise you won't be disappointed.

5. Identify and nurture your giving dream. I once had a man whose wife had died several years before say to me, "Why am I still here? Why doesn't God take me?" The answer is: because he still can be of service to others. His mission, like yours, is to find a way to be of service, to practice loving kindness, by giving to the cause that affects you most.

A woman who had two gripping encounters while mourning the deaths of loved ones shared this wisdom about her mission in life:

> There is another insight in regard to how my EEs have changed my life: I became conscious of trying to ascertain what my mission or missions in life are, and being mindful and responsible about completing them properly. In my case, I feel that my primary mission so far has been to raise my two children to the best of my ability, and to give them the gift of faith. I also feel that I have

been impressed with a need to continually grow in spiritual maturity and wisdom. I have been keeping a spiritual journal since 1992 and write down spiritual insights or thoughts of wisdom whenever I "receive" them.

What touches and stirs your heart? War-torn communities? The tears of a friend? Hungry children? Elderly people who are living alone? Those are the people you should be focusing on serving. Those are the people who should be the focus of your overall mission of giving.

6. Learn to live outside yourself. One of the best-kept secrets for dealing with any kind of emotional pain is learning to live outside yourself. What do I mean by that? Well, look at what the great American physician Dr. Karl Menninger said when asked what would be most helpful to a depressed person. His answer: Help someone more depressed. Although it may be hard at first, you'll alleviate your grief if you move beyond your own sadness and support those around you. (For example, many widows and widowers have told me they found solace in helping their grieving children.) Escape the prison of your mind and your sad thoughts by putting yourself in someone else's world for part of each day.

The Importance of Compassion

There's one thing I didn't mention above—something that you can give with hardly any effort that will have a profound effect on whoever receives it. Compassion.

Compassion is truly the forerunner of service to others. The Dali Lama, the spiritual and temporal leader of Tibet and a Nobel Prize winner, defines compassion as a "mental attitude based on the wish for others to be free of their suffering, which is associated with a sense of commitment, responsibility, and respect toward the other." He goes on to say that everyone has a fundamental right to be happy and to overcome suffering. *Compassion*, like *love*, is an action word, a call to service. It takes work, not just good intentions.

How can we practice compassion? That's a big question to answer. On the large scale, there are all the people in the world who are homeless, out of a job, desperate for food, living in squalor or despair, childless, or friendless who need our help as fellow members of the human race. But that's a topic for a different book. As mourners, specifically, we have lots of opportunities to practice being sympathetic, understanding, faithful, tender, kind, and merciful—in other words, compassionate. That's especially true when we think in terms of our own grief and what it means for us to experience the compassion of others. Reach out to other people in your community who have recently suffered a loss. Allow your own grief experiences to guide your interactions—you've been in their shoes, now help them make their way in their own grief journeys. Be compassionate within your own family and interpersonal relationships, with your spouse, children, friends, and coworkers. In the pressurized context of mourning, be mindful of the motives, influences, and experiences that may be prompting their responses to various situations. I'm referring here to things like missing appointments, making poor choices, or not doing things your way. Realizing why a person is behaving in a way you disagree with *before* you react negatively is an important exercise in compassion for mourners, one that can eliminate conflicts that eventually grow out of proportion. Remember, you have the power to choose not to take personal offense at behaviors you dislike. When you do, you'll further develop the skills of compassion—patience, understanding, respect, generosity, self-sacrifice.

We can practice compassion to ourselves, as well. Mourners need to take time daily to replenish their emotional and physical energies. When you're grieving, treat yourself as though you're your own best friend, because you are. Never feel guilty about taking care of your needs, even if those needs temporarily come before reaching out to others. As I said in the last chapter, true happiness comes from engaging in, as I call it, inner work. You'll know when you're ready to start turning outward again. And when you do, you'll find yourself in a self-sustaining cycle: Practicing compassion helps neutralize the tangled web of sadness that leads to isolation, prompting more outer-directed action. A new world will emerge as you regain your sense of control.

There's only one hazard associated with training ourselves to be compassionate: Shying away from or playing down the times when *receiving* from others is appropriate. I'm willing to bet that the one thing that will surprise you about giving is how the more you help people, the more they'll want to return your generosity. It's very important that you remain open to receiving it—remember, you're providing an opportunity for others to practice their motivation to serve. Allow them to reach out to you, to meet your needs. Don't ever think you aren't worthy. Everyone deserves to receive.

BELIEVE YOU CAN MAKE
A DIFFERENCE

No matter what loss you're mourning, or pain you're enduring, you have the power to make a difference in someone's life. Believe that your efforts are needed, regardless of your wealth or status. Even if you think you have little to give, reach out—you'll find you have more inside you than you ever knew. There are so many people who are silent about their needs, including members of your own family; so many out there grieving losses of loved ones, health, abilities, jobs, homes, or ideals. Those are the people who need you.

Let's close this chapter with a final example of how EEs can be a gift from our deceased loved ones.

My own EE happened in 1985. My father-in-law was killed in a plane crash in 1984. I was having a difficult time with his death, especially as it was getting close to Christmas (the time he died).

I smoked at the time and he disliked cigarettes. On the day my EE happened, I was on my way to buy a carton, having given up once more on quitting. As I was driving, I slowly realized he was in the passenger seat of my car. He told me he loved me and that I didn't need to buy the cigarettes. It was his Christmas gift to me.

Nevertheless, I still went and picked up the carton, thinking I had an overactive imagination. When I tried to smoke, I realized I had completely lost my taste for the things. I threw the carton away and have never had one since. It was the best Christmas gift I ever received.

—Becky Watkins, Alexandria, Louisiana

Yes, Extraordinary Encounters are precious gifts, gifts that remind us that we are loved forever. That idea is the crown jewel of the seven wisdom lessons, and the subject of the concluding chapter of this book.

You give but little when you give of your possessions.
It is when you give of yourself that you truly give.

—KAHLIL GIBRAN

CHAPTER EIGHT

YOU ARE LOVED FOREVER

*Love cures people—both the ones who give it
and the ones who receive it.*

—DR. KARL MENNINGER

At this point we've talked a great deal about ways to successfully cope with the loss of a loved one. But there's one thing we have yet to cover—something that matters tremendously to those attempting to deal with grief. Let me ask you one question: What is the most important thing you can do when confronting loss and a lifetime of change? The answer is: love.

I know. You're probably asking yourself, "How am I supposed to love when the person or people I love died?" It can be a difficult idea to understand, at first. But I'm going to try to prove to you that choosing to make love—both for your deceased loved one and for the other people in your life—a priority when you're mourning will better equip you to deal with the adverse conditions in your life. I firmly believe there is no better way to cope with the loss of a loved one than by becoming a more loving person in all that you say and do. Choosing to love will strengthen your inner life, reduce your anxiety and the intensity of your grief, lower the levels of stress hormones in your body, and help you feel better about yourself at a time when your self-esteem level is probably relatively low. Finally, and most important, loving will inevitably increase the connections that actually do the work of healing, protecting you from isolation and depression, and allowing you to reinvest your emotional energy.

Now the question is, where do you begin? How do you start the process of embracing your new world with all your heart? As the young grandmother in the next story shows, joy and happiness begin to appear when you rise above yourself.

My grandma, Gladys Mullen, personified the word ma-triarch. *She led her family through life's changes with a strength and determination no one was brave enough to question. We all loved her, and like all loving mothers, her wings expanded over us to protect us in the harshest weather, taught us to soar to our greatest heights, and* led us in directions we dared not go because of our deepest fear of the unknown.

The day the ambulance attendants carried Grandma from my parents' loving home and their personal care to the hospice facility, her heart let out a moan that announced to us all that she, too, knew fear. I never would have believed this strong-willed woman, who raised her three sons alone during an era when divorce was uncommon and shameful in some social circles, could ever be afraid. Even though her passing was imminent, her body frail with age and cancer, she was not ready to leave us. Her eyes and heart still held all her memories of life and loving her family. She was my hero. What would happen to all of us? She was our leader.

While I sat close to her on the bed at the hospital, I leaned over and kissed her cheek. I wanted so much to believe she would always be with me. My last request of her was something I had long pondered. I asked her to kiss my rosebush when she got to heaven. She had given me a rosebush, along with the other children and grandchildren; it had always been our joke that, out of everyone, after three years my bush still could not bloom.

I had never witnessed dying before, nor the mask that disguises the face as death begins to hollow the physical form we are loaned on earth. Still, I could see her soul *had not escaped her eyes as I whispered one last time that I loved her. I was not present when she finally left us that night, nor was anyone else beside her. She fought to stay until the very last moment, as if she could not accept that we had to go on in different directions. I've wondered if she waited to move on that chilly March night until she knew everyone had stepped out for a moment and no one was left to witness the inevitable. It would be just like her to protect us from her final exit.*

When she passed on, I knew she loved me. I just never realized how much the power of love could still radiate once a person's life ceased to exist in the physical form on earth. I did not doubt that my memory of her would stay forever etched in my mind. My life parallels hers. I, too, became a single woman raising three sons alone. I, too, had her determination. I, too, later married a man who never had children of his own, but raised my sons as if they were his own with the greatest love in his heart, just like Grandpa did with her family. I just did not realize she would continue to protect me, teach me, and lead me in directions whenever I was afraid to grow. Those things, however, became apparent the following May on my birthday. I was in my kitchen and, by happenstance, glanced out my window into my backyard. It was then that I witnessed my rosebush in full bloom for the very first time. She had honored our contract and had given me the most phenomenal birthday gift in my life—a heavenly blessing.

She still presents spiritual offerings, often at times when I need to find a peace within my soul. For example, the rosebush will sometimes bloom out of season. On one such occasion, my son Chad brought his friend Shannon over with a grieving heart at the passing of her grandfather. It was late November. I shared my rosebush story with her that night at the kitchen table. I wanted to provide her with peace of mind and the hope of love that lasts eternally. Shannon's greatest comfort, however, did not come from me. The next day as I was leaving for work, I glanced over at my rosebush and discovered the most beautiful bud in perfect form that had not been there the day before. I did not stop to question that this bud was blooming out of season. I stopped the car, trimmed the rose, and carried it immediately to the funeral home. Shannon's comfort that day was beyond anything any human being could have offered.

I since sold the house with Grandma's rosebush, and I struggled tremendously with leaving it behind. But an inner peace came over me and an inner voice spoke within me to let me know there would be other ways and other signs. In the harsh winter of my move, the bush might not survive a transplant, since our new home was not ready for us to move into for two months. The following spring I purchased a like rosebush the first week of May for our new home. I said my prayer as I dug the hole to plant it. As I watered it that first day, a voice from within me said, "Sue, water the roots, just as you should always water and nourish your soul." Twelve days later, on Mother's Day, my bush presented me with three gorgeous, perfect buds. One represented each of my three sons. I knew then that love would always remain and protect me.

I am now a grandmother of forty-nine years of age who has carried this memory with me for more than twenty years. My spiritual life has expanded immensely since Grandma died and communicated with me several months later. She gave me the spiritual strength to endure the experiences I was yet to face. It was through that initial spiritual contact that I began to form the beliefs that I now have; it was from that initial contact that I began to open up and listen to the deeper part of my soul for answers. We are never taught how to listen or interpret the inner messages we receive through what most people call their "gut reaction" or intuition. When our self-destructing thoughts or critiquing minds override messages we are to receive from our spiritual source,

I believe we are then directed to other people—like my grandma—who can teach us how to listen.

My grandmother's death and her spiritual message continue to influence me in the choices I make and the stories I share with others. My stories about her death have encouraged others to share their stories with me. Each one I hear renews my faith in my belief that love continues after death. And as I am sure you will agree, it is our belief system that is the driving force behind our behavior, our stresses, and our life choices. Our belief system can imprison us or set us free. Grandmother helped me change my belief system through the rose bush.

—Sue Miskell, New Berlin, Illinois

THE IMPORTANCE OF LOVE IN LIFE

Extraordinary Encounters, by nature, involve both the giving and the receiving of love. But they also function as reminders that, even though love is eternal and continues on after death, it is of absolutely no value to anyone until it is given away. That's the clear message behind every EE. Someone *gives* love to another in need with no strings attached. Someone like Sue's grandmother, who through the symbol of the rosebush, illustrated the transforming power of love on life. And Sue, in turn, gave the same gift of love and reassurance to other mourners in need. In that way Sue's grandmother began a cycle of love and belief that would be passed on from family to family, generation to generation.

I believe love is actually a *decision* to bring happiness, peace, and healing to another. And the proof of that decision is being able to act in a loving way, even as we're putting our comfort and preferences in second place (a fact that all loving relationships can attest to). As we all know, it can hurt to do the loving thing. But being loved, like experiencing the extraordinary, makes us feel valued again. The reason Extraordinary Encounters are so helpful to the bereaved is because they meet two of our most basic human needs: affirmation and connection. EEs make clear that we are always important to the person who died, and reaffirm that love is the one thing we take with us into eternity. Loving relationships—loving, and being loved in return—are at the very heart of psychological and emotional health because they reinforce those feelings of value and connection. It's through that interdependence that we get a sense of our mutual importance.

Many years ago I heard the famous author and surgeon, Dr. Bernie Siegel, say that love was the most powerful immune stimulant known to medicine. Of course, at the time, that statement raised many an eyebrow in the medical community. But I saw the truth of Siegel's statement in my work with the dying. I remember when the attending physician told the first patient in our hospice that he had six months to live. During those next six months, the patient, Gerald, received so much loving care from the nurses, volunteers, and one physician's assistant that his death sentence came and went—literally. He lived. And he was furious at his doctor for causing him a lot of anxiety about his approaching death. Consequently he not only got out of his bed, but also even drove his truck again. I took a walk with him on the land near his home and saw the repair jobs he had started and completed. He lived another year because of the love freely given by his care team. Since then, further research has shown that dying people who have a strong loving support system do live longer than those who have been abandoned or have no immediate family or friends who visit and give support, backing up Siegel's claim.

Of course, it's difficult to give away something you don't feel you have. There are many people who weren't brought up in loving environments, who never heard mothers, fathers, or relatives saying, "I love you." But remember, you're not required to act like your mother, father, or any other relative. You *can* learn to be more loving. To that end, one of the most important things you can do is to follow the example of people who are living examples of forgiveness, caring, affection, trust, generosity, and approval. Think of the people in your life and the ways they express their love. Whenever possible, model your behavior—the way you act, speak to others, give thanks, even the way you smile—after theirs. Another important thing is to do what we talked about in Chapter 7: giving. Recognizing and filling needs, being thoughtful, caring, and kind, is the precursor to loving well.

Beyond those general suggestions, here are some simple steps to help you learn how to love unconditionally:

1. **Do small works of love.** Small deeds of love can have a big impact on the recipient. Offer to help change a flat tire; make a telephone call in the evening to a widow dealing with loneliness; provide transportation for someone who does not have an automobile; bring home a surprise treat for after dinner. Simply say "I trust you" to a friend, coworker, or a family member. Simone Weil, the French mystic, says the fullness of love simply means being able to say to another, "What are you going through?" I promise, if you look for them, you'll find potential works of love all around you.

2. Practice not expecting anything in return for a good deed. It can be difficult to do at times, but you will grow immensely as a loving person if you can avoid giving conditionally. That means loving with no expectation of return. No money. No goods. No return favors. No invites back. That is perfect love—no demands, no trades. Do everything in your power not to put conditions on your feelings, and beware of the trap of being satisfied with your ability to love. Practice going deeper.

3. Carry on the love and traditions of your deceased loved ones. Begin by letting others know it's okay with you to talk about the deceased—they should feel free to bring them up in conversations. Then, take time to think about the love and the lessons you learned from the person who died. That love is still present among those still living, including you. Are you carrying that love and experience forward in your work and with your family? Are you talking about it with friends and family? Consider ways you can implement that love in your life.

As for carrying on the traditions of your loved one, there are no criteria. Think of where you used to go with your loved one or something he or she always urged you to do. Turn it into a tradition by doing it regularly (daily, monthly, or yearly—it doesn't matter). It could be a fall outing to see the leaves change, a trip to a favorite restaurant, or deciding to visit all of the capitol cities in the United States. You can also pick up one of your loved one's hobbies. Use it as a way to express your love for the deceased, and to remind you of the unconditional love you share. And remember, it's okay to let go of traditions that bring pain or turn out not to contribute to your new life. Transform them as you see fit; if that fails, abandon them entirely and try something else.

4. Do a daily love review. How can you live the truth that you are loved forever? The answer is by being sure you *give and receive love each day*. Before you drop off to sleep at night, ask yourself two simple questions: "When during the day did I willingly give or receive unconditional love?" Review the scene in detail. Focus on the people involved and what was said and done. Those thoughts alone will improve your mental and emotional health.

Next, ask yourself, "When did I fail to give and receive love, and how can I do better next time?" Think about how you can increase your ability to be more loving, and also how you limit the loving opportunities of others. Decide what you'll do the following day to improve your ability to give joy and receive the comforting presence of friends and family. Don't wait for others to be loving—

start loving first. Think of this daily love review as another way to honor the deceased who gave so much to you. If you practice this self-questioning, you'll heighten your awareness and ability to love and be loved.

5. Live as though everything in your life is on loan. Have you ever considered that the food, clothing, or shelter you consider "yours" are really on loan from the universe? Have you ever thought about our time on earth not as a right, but as an opportunity to accept the gifts of life and love? Making that mental shift—thinking about everything you own as a gift—makes it so much easier to let things go, to avoid making the mundane the centerpiece of your life. The next time something makes you angry or frustrated, take a step back and remind yourself that it's a gift just to be breathing in and out at that moment. Believe me when I say that living with that kind of freedom from attachment will make it much easier to give and receive freely.

6. Counter rejection with love. This is a monumental task, but one that is vital to the grief process. Rejection can be a deep and painful wound. In fact, there are few other experiences that challenge the power of unconditional love so strongly—once we've been turned away, it becomes that much harder for us to risk our hearts again. But I beg you, don't let rejection make you afraid to love. Instead, try to use it to increase your insight and awareness and continue to move forward. If you've been holding on to the pangs of rejection that the death of your loved one brought alive in you, decide right now to let your bitterness go. Make a list of all the ways you can love him or her in separation (see Step Three in this list). Remember, there are so many more people in the world who need your love right at this moment. You can't afford to stop reaching out.

7. **Learn to recognize the signs of Heart Wisdom.** In *The Little Prince*, French author Antoine de Saint-Exupery says that "It is only with the heart that one can see rightly; what is essential is invisible to the eye." The philosopher Pascal observed, "The heart has reasons which reason cannot know." The point of those two statements? When you're making important choices, especially about weighty problems, you must always listen to your heart as well as your reason and intellect. I believe getting in touch with that inner Heart Wisdom, that loving guidance, is how we find the Higher Power within us. Wisdom really can come in a flash, when love is the force behind it; heart messages can come in the form of visions, nature and animals, dreams, people (strangers or friends), poetry, songs, or

readings. Be alert for and pay attention to the signs. Listen with your heart to what comes up within you as you ponder a problem and ask for advice. Your inner guidance won't lie to you.

8. Always be humble. In my experience a person with a pure heart has two major characteristics: humility and the intent to do what he or she believes is right. Be assured, there are few virtues more important than humility for interacting with and understanding those in need. In a larger sense humility is one of the defining characteristics of EEs, both in terms of the giver (an unseen love acting purely out of concern for the recipient), and the receiver (in terms of putting our intellect behind us for a moment and accepting the mysteries of the universe). Deepak Chopra, physician and bestselling author, said in *The Seven Spiritual Laws of Success*, "It is the intention behind your giving and receiving that is the most important thing." Your intent to do right will be manifested in what you do with your EE, how you receive and use it—ideally, for you own good and also out of your love for others. Remember, EEs are not just for the benefit of mourners, but for family and friends as well.

Learning to Love in Separation

We've talked about the importance of establishing a new relationship with your deceased loved one through memory, ritual, and tradition. But in the context of this chapter—in the context of the idea of unconditional, everlasting love—I want to frame the idea in a different way. When you're establishing your new relationship with the deceased, what you're really doing is becoming an expert at loving in separation. After all, that's what EEs really tell us—that those who have gone before us have taken their love into the realm of eternity and are still sharing it. And as I've said, it's your responsibility to reciprocate and give back; to spread that love to the people around you.

How you decide to express your love in separation depends on your unique relationship with the deceased, your beliefs and creativity, and your willingness to explore. Here are some of the ways other mourners have told me they continue to give and receive love. Feel free to adapt them to your situation, and add some of your own.

- My daughters and I made a memory box of mementos for the grandchildren that describe their grandfather.

- I make it a point to talk to him out loud.

- I started a journal, let him know what was bothering me, and asked for permission to move on.

- I started a new tradition in his memory.

- I collected memories by asking family and friends, young and old, as well as former coworkers, to write what they remembered about him at different times in his life. I tried to get remembrances from three different generations.

- I wrote down my favorite memories of her and read them aloud when I was alone, or on appropriate occasions.

- I routinely read a verse from Scripture that presents me with a vivid reminder of him.

- I visit the favorite places we used to go and think about her.

- I wrote a history of our relationship that I will give to my son.

- I pray to him to help me deal with certain issues.

- When we sit around the table, I ask each person if

they would say something they remember about my husband.

- Because he loved music, I started a scholarship fund in his name at the Florida West Coast Symphony Orchestra.

- On the anniversary of his death, we go out for dinner in his honor.

- I ask him to visit me in a dream.

As you can see, there's no right or wrong way to express your love in separation—you can do it each day or on special days, alone or in the company of others. It all depends on your vision and needs. And it all starts with a decision to open your heart back up after your loss.

Some time ago I asked Anne (the social worker you met in Chapter 2), what she learned from her Extraordinary Encounters that might help other people live more fulfilling lives. Her answer, which follows, is a model for how you can decide to become an expert in loving in separation.

What I have learned from my EEs is somewhat difficult to verbalize. I think the main thing is that we continue in some form after death, and whatever that form is, we still have both self-identity and recognition of those we love. Our selfhood continues. Also, I believe my experience was the deepest gift based on my relationship with Jenny. She had deep spiritual beliefs, and the discussions we had as I was growing up about God, relationships, love, values, etc., were significant for both of us. The gift of love she gave to me as she left this world was the knowledge that there is life after death. I think that is what we all wonder about, worry about, look forward to, etc. She also taught me about the eternity of love. My personal belief is that God loves each of us unconditionally as his/her children and wants us to share that love. My EEs have felt supportive of that belief. I think what I would like to share with others is that love is eternal and that who we are has very little to do with our physical bodies and everything to do with our soul/spirit and how we share our love.

As Anne's story illustrates, the major lesson of the Extraordinary Encounter is that love, evolving and ongoing, is the ultimate force behind adapting to loss and change. There is no stronger healing force. We owe much to our deceased loved ones, who through optimism, determination, and affection provide us with this love, this

YOU ARE LOVED FOREVER

essential link to health and well-being. As playwright Thornton Wilder writes at the end of his novel, *The Bridge of San Luis Rey*, "There is a land of the living and a land of the dead. The bridge is love; the only truth, the only survival."

Increasing your ability to love in separation will allow you to accomplish three important tasks in the grief process: to live with freedom, renew your love daily, and accept inevitable change.

1. Live with freedom. Freedom is inherent to love, because love does not control or possess; it is eternally accepting. And the love given to us by our deceased loved ones always extends the freedom to grieve according to our individual needs, to grow at our own pace. I believe there are few mistakes greater than demanding conformity—holding on too tightly, wanting another to "do as I do" or "grieve as I grieve." Those kinds of demands smother and strangle love. Ask yourself: *Are you trying to control someone due to the loss you are experiencing, possibly a friend, counselor, or coworker?* Or is someone trying to control how you express your grief? If the answer is yes, make the choice to put a stop to it, right away. Remember, when you're mourning, you can't assume those around you know what you need. You might have to remind them you have the right to grieve as you wish, free and unencumbered by their expectations. Keep in mind, that also means allowing others in your family to grieve in their own individual ways. You'll find that kind of freedom sets the stage for renewed hope and optimism.

2. Renew your love daily. Love not only gives mourners the freedom to travel different paths, it accepts others as they are. That's where the commitment to a daily renewal of love comes in. Love begins with forgiveness and a fresh start each day, releasing the previous day's conflicts or negative experiences. Something as seemingly mundane as letting go of what happened yesterday at the funeral or the cemetery, or something said in poor taste at the wake, can become an important spiritual practice that will enhance your ability to cope with change. Love realizes that the person you are forgiving is just like you—human, and able to make mistakes.

Disillusionment is painful, but is also a reminder of our humanity. It reminds us of the need to give second chances and let go of grudges, which sap energy and destroy inner peace. It's a fact of life—people don't always live up to our expectations. But when you practice a daily renewal of love, you'll allow yourself to relate to people as though every encounter is the first encounter. Both of you will become stronger emotionally, and more able to love unconditionally.

3. Accept inevitable change. Love recognizes that change is perpetual—loved ones change their interests, mindsets, and of course, change physically. Nothing stays the same. Your relationships with them will change dramatically, as well. Friends you thought you could count on may change in ways you dislike; on the other hand, you might find yourself growing closer to someone you'd never felt close to. Try to remember, they're not the only ones who are changing—you will not be the same person you were before your loved one died. Everyone has to adjust and accept change. The key is resolving to do the best you can with the new conditions you face, and *not resisting them*. Change always wins. Let love give you the courage to undertake a journey of change, and watch as a different "you" emerges from your grief work.

THE PARADOXES OF LOVE

It's both a joyful and a tragic fact that loss is an integral part of loving. When we choose to love at any stage in life, at the very same moment (and probably unknowingly), we choose to grieve the eventual loss of that loved one. In that way grief is a paradoxical payback for loving well. But as we have seen, love is eternally renewed through Extraordinary Encounters, just as grief is tempered by our knowledge of continuity. Our ability to "forget" past injuries and really live the three love characteristics—freedom, renewal, and acceptance—allows us to heal completely even as we reach out to those around us.

It's no easy task to focus on the fulfillment of the other. Nevertheless, true lovers are first and foremost guided by selflessness. If you give love without conditions, eventually it returns, but—and here's the second paradox—only if you don't actively pursue it. You can't seek to be loved. All you can do is open your heart to those around you—including those who have died—and when you least expect it, love will find you.

Don't believe me? Just read this story. . . .

My mother passed away on November 5, 2001, from Alzheimer's disease. I was with her when she passed and had the presence of mind to ask her to please give me a sign, if she could, that she was okay. I waited and waited for a sign, which never came. Finally, when I was least expecting it, I received one.

One year after she died, I was planning to go to Sa-

vannah for a short vacation over the Thanksgiving holiday. The weekend before I was supposed to leave, I was at home packing for my trip. On Saturday, around two or three in the afternoon, I walked from my den through the formal dining room, a room that my mother loved, on my way to the kitchen. (When I used to bring my mom to my house, she would comment, "It's pretty in here.") I passed by a chair, where I saw my mother sitting as she always sat, ankles crossed, left arm across her stomach, and the other arm upright with her face leaning on her hand. It was so natural to see her like that, I just acknowledged calmly to myself, "Oh, there's Mom." The image was colorless, though her hair and blouse were darker than her white pants and shoes. She looked like she did before she got sick, whole and healthy. When I got to the kitchen and it began to sink in as to what I had just seen, I walked back to look at the chair, and there was nothing there.

I felt that I had finally been given the sign I had asked my mom to send. I felt extremely privileged to have had the experience. Since then, I have relaxed in my grieving process, although I still miss her. The experience has given me reassurance. My mother and I were very close. I took care of her for six years, and I was at her side to see her take her last breath. I feel the experi-

ence was a way for my mom to let me know that she was "okay." November had been a difficult month for me, as I remembered the struggle with the disease until her death. I believe the visit from my mom was a gift of comfort and love, and a way of saying hello and good-bye. I miss my mother every day, but I think the experience marked her passing, and has allowed a resolution of sorts. I feel that she is still around me, even though I can't see her. I think that is what she was communicating to me—that she still "exists." I believe strongly that there is so much more to life than what we can see.

—Donna McDermott, Norcross, Georgia

I started this chapter by saying that love never fails—never fails to give us the power to cope effectively with major losses, to deal with the life changes that result, and finally to spread the same love to those around us. Remember, somewhere, at this very moment, someone is in need of your love. And there isn't a person alive who can't, in some small and humble way, fill the need for love in someone who feels empty and unimportant.

The continued sense of joy, peace, and security you'll get from widening your circle of love will take you to a place inside that you never thought existed—a place of indescribable beauty and insight. As you emerge from your difficult loss, wherever you are in your ability to love, know that you can go higher and higher. Don't waste a single day.

I end this chapter with more from Diana Sautelle, whom you met in Chapter 3, and whose childhood experience after the death of her friend Ernie heavily influenced her entire life.

Ever since Ernie came to me in Spirit, I have known about the power of love, and that connections of love go beyond life and into the realms of death/Spirit. I know that this experience is possible for anyone, and everyone. All people carry within them an immortal soul and are connected to one another and to Spirit through love. I will always speak from my heart directly to another's heart. I do not hide my soul and I send love to all other's souls, whether they are serving me over the counter, or working as musicians on my compositions.

Diana's comments speak to the belief that our lives are truly journeys of and to wholeness. Spirit is, as Einstein wrote, "the invisible piper to whose mysterious tone human beings, vegetables, and cosmic dust dance." So remember, we never dance alone. The world of the unseen is all around us, providing insights for living; we only have to be receptive to the music of the universe that directs it all.

Perhaps we all need to be reminded of an observation from Greek author Nikos Kazantzakis: "The highest point a person can attain is not knowledge, or virtue, or goodness, or victory, but something even greater, more heroic . . . sacred awe." Awe is a natural response to mystery, mystery that introduces itself into our lives through Extraordinary Encounters. Words alone don't describe this reality. How will you respond when it comes to you? I hope you will be able to make the decision to trust your inner wisdom, accept the changes that life keeps demanding, and always remember that it's action, experiences— what you do—and above all, the gift of love, that allow you to integrate your loss into the next chapter of your life.

I wish you only the best in creating life after loss.

❧

Everyone has inside of him a piece of good news.
The good news is that you don't know how great you
can be. How much you can love! What you can
accomplish! And what your potential is!

—ANNE FRANK, 1929–1945

APPENDIX A

SUGGESTED READINGS ON EXTRAORDINARY ENCOUNTERS

Amatuzio, Janis. *Forever Ours*. Midwest Forensic Pathology, P.A. 3960 Coon Rapids Blvd., LL21, Coon Rapids, MN 54433, 2002.

Anderson, Joan Wester. *Where Miracles Happen*. New York: Brett Books, 1994.

Anderson, Megory. "Facing the Other Side." *Spirituality & Health*, Winter 2003.

Arcangel, D. *Afterlife Encounters*. Charlottesville, VA: Hampton Roads, 2005.

Botkin, A. *Induced After-Death Communication*. Charlottesville, VA: Hampton Roads, 2005.

Bramblett, J. *When Goodbye Is Forever: Learning to Live Again After the Loss of a Child*. New York: Ballantine Books, 1991. (See pages 147–157.)

Browning, Sinclair. *Feathers Brush My Heart*. New York: Warner Books, 2002.

Cardena, E., Lynn, S., Krippner, S. (eds.). *Varieties of Anomalous Experience: Examining the Scientific Evidence*. Washington, DC: American Psychological Association, 2000.

Devers, Edie. "Experiencing the Deceased." *Florida Nursing Review, 2* (Jan. 1988): 7–13.

———. *Goodbye Again: Experiences with Departed Loved Ones*. Kansas City: Andrews & McMeel, 1997.

Duminiak, Christine. *God's Gift of Love: After-Death Communications*. Xlibris Corporation: www.Xlibris.com, 2003.

Eliach, Yaffa. *Hasidic Tales of the Holocaust*. New York: Oxford University Press, 1982. (See pages 39–41, 169–172.)

Finley, Mitch. *Whispers of Love: Encounters with Deceased Relatives and Friends*. New York: Crossroads, 1995.

Fisher, Helen. *From Erin with Love*. Bend, OR: Swallowtail Publishing, 1995.

Fontana, D. *Is There an Afterlife?* Arlesford, U.K.: John Hunt, 2005.

Garfield, P. *The Dream Messenger*. New York: Simon & Schuster, 1997.

Greer, Jane. *The Afterlife Connection*. New York: St. Martin's Press, 2003.

Guggenheim, W. & Guggenheim, J. *Hello from Heaven*. New York: Bantam, 1996.

Haraldsson, Erlendur. "The Iyengar-Kirti Case: An Apparitional Case of the Bystander Type," *Journal of the Society for Psychical Research* (1987): 54, No. 806.

Honigman, A. (ed.). *My Proof of Survival: Personal Accounts of Contact with the Hereafter*. St. Paul, MN: Llewellyn, 2004.

Hurley, Tom. "Dwelling with the Mystery of Death." *Noetic Sciences Review* (Spring 1994): 6–7.

Inglis, Brian. *Coincidences: A Matter of Chance—Or Synchronicity?* London: Hutchinson, 1990.

Jung, Carl. *Memories, Dreams, Reflections*. New York: Vintage Books, 1965. (See pages 312–314.)

Kastenbaum, Robert. *Is There Life After Death?* London: Multimedia Books Limited, 1995. (See pages 90–96.)

Kübler-Ross, Elisabeth. *Death Is of Vital Importance*. Barrytown, NY: Station Hill Press, 1995. (See pages 95–98.)

LaGrand, L. *After Death Communication: Final Farewells*. St. Paul, MN: Llewellyn Publications, 1997.

———. "Are We Missing Opportunities to Help the Bereaved?" *The Forum Newsletter*, Vol. 23 (Sept./Oct. 1997): 5.

———. "Extraordinary Experiences of the Bereaved." *The Psi Researcher* (Nov. 1996) No. 23: 8–11.

———. *Gifts from the Unknown*. New York: Authors Choice Press, 2001.

———. "Incorporating the Extraordinary Experiences of the Bereaved into Personal Rituals," *The Forum*, Vol. 31, 4 (Oct./Nov./Dec. 2005): 6.

———. *Messages and Miracles: The Extraordinary Experiences of the Bereaved*. St. Paul, MN: Llewellyn Publications, 1999.

———. "The Nature and Therapeutic Implications of the Extraordinary Experiences of the Bereaved," *Journal of Near-Death Studies* (Nov. 2005).

Lawson, L. *Visitations from the Afterlife*. San Francisco: HarperSanFrancisco, 2000.

Lewis, C. S. *A Grief Observed*. New York: Bantam, 1980. (See pages 85–87.)

Millman, D. & Childers, D. *Divine Interventions*. Emmaus, PA: Daybreak Books, 1999.

Morrell, D. *Fireflies*. New York: E.P. Dutton, 1988. (See pages 33–47.)

Radin, Dean. *The Conscious Universe: The Scientific Truth of Psychic Phenomena*. San Francisco: Harper Edge, 1997.

Sayers, Dorothy. *Introduction to Dante: The Divine Comedy: Paradise III*. New York: Penguin Classics, 1962. (See pages 35–37.)

Rushnell, Squire. *When God Winks*. Hillsboro, OR: Beyond Words Publishing, Inc., 2001.

Sparrow, Scott. *I Am Always with You*. New York: Bantam, 1995.

Treece, Patricia. *Messengers: After-Death Appearances of Saints and Mystics*. Huntington, IN: Our Sunday Visitor Publishing Division, 1995.

White, Rhea (ed.). *Exceptional Human Experience: Special Issue*. New Bern, NC: The Exceptional Human Experience Network, 1997.

Woods, Kay. *Visions of the Bereaved*. Pittsburgh: Sterling House, 1998.

Wright, S. "Experiences of Spontaneous Psychokinesis After Bereavement," *Journal of the Society for Psychical Research* (July 1998), Vol.62, No. 852.

Wright, S. *When Spirits Come Calling*. Nevada City, CA: Blue Dolphin, 2002.

NINE PROVEN SURVIVAL SKILLS FOR COPING WITH LOSS AND CHANGE

Although the world is full of suffering, it is full also of the overcoming of it.

—HELEN KELLER

I. COMMUNICATE AND RELATE

Find someone you trust to talk to about what you are thinking and feeling. It could be a friend, relative, neighbor, professional, support group, your loved one, or God. Talking is a well-accepted way of reaching out for help, so tell someone about your pain, the emptiness and the emotions you are struggling with, what you miss, and how the loss has affected your thinking. It's okay to repeat yourself for a while—repetition leads to healing—but constant dwelling on sadness reinforces it in your long-term memory. Also, talk about what you think you should do to get through your grief. Listen to those who have gone before you or are ahead of you in dealing with loss—then ask questions. Since grief emotions tend to be isolating, it is important to reach out and find someone with whom you can let your emotional defenses down. If you are not ready to talk to others, at the very least, talk to yourself out loud about your feelings.

2. DISCOVER AND GRIEVE YOUR SECONDARY LOSSES

There are usually a number of secondary or associated losses connected to your major loss that go unrecognized. They might include having to move to a smaller house, financial hardship, loss of a confidant or a sexual partner, or the loss of a dream about the future together. Loss of meaning is a big, and often overlooked, secondary loss. Identify these losses—some of which might come months or years later—and grieve them as you would any physical loss. Talk about them and what they mean to you.

3. EXPRESS YOUR EMOTIONS

Take the opportunity to express what you are feeling when you find yourself suddenly overwhelmed with sad thoughts. Shed the ingrained cultural belief that showing emotion is a sign of weakness. Believe me, it will be physiologically and psychologically releasing to freely mourn. Crying is coping and healthy. If you can't cry or don't feel like crying, then consider writing, drawing, or painting what you are feeling. Allow yourself the freedom to express what is happening inside you.

4. TAKE ACTION

When you are inactive and feeling down, go ahead and allow yourself to feel a tiny bit of pity—then immediately take action. Get up; do something, anything to change your physiology and your focus. Go outside for a walk, to shop, or to rake the yard. Never allow yourself to stay in an inactive self-pitying state. All healthy coping begins with a choice to change your attitude when dealing with your loss. You *can* choose to change your present circumstances, if only temporarily.

5. START NEW ROUTINES AND TRADITIONS

You are building a new life as a result of your loss, and new routines are a necessity for firmly establishing that life. Stay away from and stop anticipating the old routines that emphasize your loss and continually remind you of your heartache. You can go back to them when you are stronger. Start new traditions that honor your loved one and highlight positive memories; or transform the old traditions by trying new approaches or involving new friends. Make the new ones second nature to you, even as you maintain the central meaning of the tradition you are preserving.

6. GO OUTSIDE OF YOURSELF

Take your attention off yourself and see what you can do to help others. With each passing day you gain new strength, experience, and knowledge that can be used in providing support for others in situations like your own. Look for someone in need. Take care of a pet for a vacationing neighbor; give a homeless person something to eat; read to someone who is recovering from an illness. Find a way *to use your skills in the service of others and increase your ability to love.* Love through service is the key to surviving loss.

7. Trust Mystery and the Unseen

Look for the coincidences that appear at just the right time during your grieving that give you comfort and remind you that you are not alone. They *will occur* when you most need them. This also means consciously paying more attention to your intuitive self. Listen to what you feel and hear inside when it comes to making decisions, when you sense the presence of your loved one, or have a special dream. Make every effort to be open to mystery and the unseen. Look for a connection to what is beyond conventional knowledge, whether you call that entity nature, the cosmos, or a Higher Power. Use the wisdom of the unseen to restructure your world view and to cope with the adjustments associated with loss.

8. REPLENISH

Physical feelings, especially fatigue, influence your emotions. Take at least a twenty-minute stress break every day. Lie down and elevate your feet; use a breathing technique, audiotape, or imagery for relaxation. Also set aside time to find spiritual replenishment: Spend time in nature, read something inspirational, start writing a history of the relationship with your loved one, or go to a quiet place for prayer. Drink at least a quart of water during the day and be sure to eat a green salad. Show compassion to yourself with quality self-care each day.

9. LEARN TO SHIFT YOUR INNER FOCUS

Become an expert at shifting the focus of your attention from painful or anxiety-producing thoughts to relaxing and or loving thoughts. This is an essential, life-affirming skill you can develop with practice—and use for the rest of your life in many stressful situations. Develop written, symbolic, or verbal (affirmations and self-talk) reminders that will change your focus and control your behavior. Try playing your favorite music. Deliberately shift your consciousness through a meditation or a prayer. Through trial and error, you'll find you'll create a technique to help you refocus when you wake up and can't get back to sleep during the night, or when you're thinking too much about your painful loss.

MYTHS ABOUT GRIEF AND GRIEF WORK

1. Grief and mourning are the same experience. Mourning is the outward expression of grief. Grief is the inescapable individual inner response to a loss. Everyone grieves, but for various reasons, some very unhealthy, not everyone mourns.

2. Grief is a two- or three-month experience (some believe two or three weeks). In reality, grief is not time bound. It can and does revisit people at various times and with various intensities. Some mourners report that the second year of their grief was worse than the first.

3. We only grieve deaths. Grief can accompany any loss experience, from divorce to the incarceration of a loved one. Much grief goes unrecognized, especially when it comes to openly mourning secondary losses or the loss of pets.

4. There is an orderly and predictable stage-like progression to the grief process. Grieving is highly individual; no two people grieve the same way. We each revisit different thoughts and experiences. Grief is like a roller-coaster, up one hour, down the next, or as C. S. Lewis wrote, it is "like a circular trench." You might think you're past one phase, but then suddenly it appears again.

5. Only family members and close friends grieve the death of a particular person. In fact, anyone who has had an emotional attachment to the deceased will grieve. This often includes caregivers, volunteers, and medical personnel. We often grieve for people we have not personally met but have read about or admired due to their public service.

6. Grief is solely an emotional response. Grief is actually manifested in a variety of ways: physically, spiritually, cognitively, and behaviorally. Confusion, forgetfulness, and fatigue are all associated with the grief process. Some people are drawn closer to their spiritual beliefs, others drift away from them.

7. It is best to try not to think about your grief and confront the pain. Facing the pain and moving toward an outward expression of what is happening inside is a good thing. Moving toward the pain leads to eventual healing. Avoiding pain causes it to resurface in many unexpected ways.

8. The goal of mourning is to be your old self again. We are never like we were before the death of our loved one because a part of us has died. For a time, life feels uncertain and different without the one who has died. We are starting a new chapter in life, learning to integrate the loss into our new world.

9. Good grief is letting go of the person who died and getting on with life. We always have a relationship with the person who died based on memory, expectation, and the lessons he or she taught us. Part of grief work is establishing that new relationship and finding ways to memorialize and appreciate the person.

10. Crying is a sign of weakness. Crying is the normal human response to any meaningful loss. It is a natural coping response that gives expression to built-up emotions and releases many of the toxic chemicals created by the stress response.

11. Grief eventually comes to an end. Grief is an adaptive response, so in reality we learn to live with the absence of our loved ones. And surely, some grief is naturally resurrected on occasion when a poignant reminder comes to our attention. It is normal for grief to revisit months or years later.

12. A person should only grieve in privacy. We all need opportunities to talk about our loved ones and the way they influenced our lives. These times will often be accompanied by tears and emotion. Because memories are potent grieving tools, the opportunity to express emotion associated with those memories is healthy and a source of healing.

BIBLIOGRAPHY

Attig, Thomas. *The Heart of Grief.* New York: Oxford University Press, 2000.

Browning, Sinclair. *Feathers Brush My Heart.* New York: Warner Books, 2002

Bulkeley, Kelly. *Spiritual Dreaming.* Mahwah, NJ: Paulist Press, 1995.

Cook, John. *The Book of Positive Quotations.* Minneapolis: Fairview Press, 1997.

Cook, R., Grayson, B. & Stevenson, I. "Do Any Near-Death Experiences Provide Evidence for the Survival of Human Personality After Death?" *Journal of Scientific Exploration,* 12, 377–406, 1998.

De Becker, Gavin. *The Gift of Fear.* New York: Dell, 1997.

DeSpelder, Lynne Ann and Strickland, Albert Lee. *The Last Dance.* Palo Alto, CA: Mayfield Publishing, 1995.

Dossey, Larry. *Healing Words.* San Francisco: HarperSanFrancisco, 1993.

———. *Prayer Is Good Medicine.* San Francisco: HarperSanFrancisco, 1996.

Fontana, David. *Is There an Afterlife?* Hants, U.K.: O Books, 2005.

Griffin, David Ray. *Parapsychology, Philosophy, and Spirituality.* Albany, NY: SUNY Press, 1997.

Grossman, Neal. "My Beliefs About Life After Death," *The Journal of Religion and Psychical Research*, Vol. 27, No. 1, January, 2004.

Grosso, Michael. *Experiencing the Next World Now*. New York: Pocket Books, 2004.

Hart, Tobin. *The Secret Spiritual World of Children*. Makawao, Maui, HI: Inner Ocean Publishing, 2003.

Honorton, Charles. "The Impoverished State of Skepticism," *The Journal of Parapsychology*, Vol. 57, June, 1993.

Kaufman, Barry. *Happiness Is a Choice*. New York: Fawcett Columbine, 1991.

LaGrand, Louis. *After Death Communication*. St. Paul, MN: Llewellyn, 1997.

———. *Gifts from the Unknown*. New York: Authors Choice Press, 2001.

———. *Messages and Miracles*. St. Paul, MN: Llewellyn, 1999.

Lama, His Holiness the Dalai & Cutler, Howard. *The Art of Happiness*. New York: Riverhead, 1998.

Lewis, C. S. *Miracles*. HarperCollins Edition, New York: Harper-Collins, 2001.

Luks, Allan. *The Healing Power of Doing Good*. New York: Authors Choice Press, 2001.

Morris, Virginia. *Talking About Death Won't Kill You*. New York: Workman, 2001.

Morse, Don. *Searching for Eternity: A Scientist's Spiritual Journey to Overcome Death Anxiety*. Memphis, Tennessee: Eagle Wing Books, Inc., 2000.

Morse, Melvin. *Where God Lives*. New York: Cliff Street Books, 2000.

Myers, F.W.H. *Human Personality and its Survival of Bodily Death*. New Hyde Park, New York: University Books, 1961.

Radin, Dean. *The Unconscious Universe: The Scientific Truth of Psychic Phenomena*. San Francisco: HarperEdge, 1997.

Raymo, Chester. *Honey from Stone*. St. Paul, MN: Ruminator Books, reprint ed., 1997.

Sarno, John. *Healing Back Pain.* New York: Warner Books, 1991.

————. *The Mindbody Prescription.* New York: Warner, 1998.

Schwartz, Gary. *The Afterlife Experiments.* New York: Atria Books, 2002.

Seligman, Martin. *Authentic Happiness.* New York: Free Press, 2002.

Stoney, Catherine. "Acute Psychological Stress Reduces Plasma Triglyceride Clearance," *Psychophysiology,* February 2002, Cambridge University Press.

Tart, Charles (Ed). *Body Mind Spirit.* Charlottesville, VA: Hampton Roads Publishing Company, Inc., 1997.

Utts, J. "An assessment of the evidence for psychic functioning". *Journal of Parapsychology,* 59, 289–320, (1995).

Vanaucken, Sheldon. *A Severe Mercy.* New York: Harper & Row, 1977.

Williamson, Marianne. *A Return to Love.* New York: HarperCollins, 1992.

Worden, J. William. *Grief Counseling and Grief Therapy.* New York: Springer, 2001.

Zeller, Max. *The Dream: The Vision of the Night.* Boston: Sigo Press, 1990.

Author's Request

If you have had an Extraordinary Encounter when mourning and would be willing to share it for possible use in helping others and in a future publication, please send it to me at the address below, e-mail it to BL450@msn.com, or send it through my website, www.extraordinarygriefexperiences.com. I would also like to hear from you about how you have used your EE to cope with your loss and how it has influenced how you look at life.

Louis LaGrand
Loss Education Associates
450 Fairway Isles Drive
Venice, Florida 34285

Louis LaGrand, Ph.D., has been teaching about death and counseling the bereaved for more than twenty-five years. A graduate of Cortland College, he is a former distinguished service professor emeritus at SUNY-Potsdam (where he started the first college course on death and bereavement), and one of the founders and past president of the Hospice of St. Lawrence Valley. A certified grief counselor, he is currently the bereavement coordinator at Our Lady of Lourdes Church and Director of Loss Education Associates in Venice, Florida. He has authored several books and numerous articles on grief, is a sought-after international speaker, and is known worldwide for his research into the afterlife experiences of the bereaved. Visit his website at www.extraordinarygriefexperiences.com.